Abbas Schirmohammadi

WORKS Vol. 5

Abbas Schirmohammadi

WORKS Vol. 5

Mein ultimatives Song Lyrics Archiv

WORKS Vol. 5

Abbas Schirmohammadi

Inhaltsverzeichnis

Vorwort

Musik ist mein Leben. Das Klavier und die Gitarre sind meine besten Freunde. Bereits als 4-jähriger Knirps durfte ich am frühkindlichen Musikunterricht teilnehmen und entwickelte schnell eine große Leidenschaft für Takt, Rhythmus und Melodie. Anstatt sich ein neues Auto anzuschaffen, kauften mir meine Eltern damals auf Empfehlung meiner Klavierlehrerin ein nagelneues ED Seiler Klavier, das ich bis heute habe.

Als 7-Jähriger kam Schlagzeugunterricht auf einem eigenen Sabian & Remo Drumset dazu. Das Kinderzimmer war ab sofort ein Musikzimmer. Ich wurde von meinen Lehrern als „überaus begabt" bezeichnet und sehr gefördert. Schon mit 10 spielte ich komplizierte Werke der Klassik rauf und runter: Beethoven, Mozart, Schubert, Vivaldi und Verdi waren meine Favoriten.

Auch mein jüngerer Bruder hatte das Musik-Gen in sich, und so musizierten wir oft gemeinsam stundenlang. Mit 14 gefiel mir die Musik von Roxette, diese Songs wollte ich unbedingt spielen. Mein Klavierlehrer war davon zuerst nicht sonderlich begeistert, doch schließlich willigte er ein, dass wir uns auch mit modernerer Musik beschäftigten.

So lernte ich, ABBA, Beatles, Roxette, David Hasselhoff, EAV, OMD, Status Quo und sonstige Musik, die ich Anfang der 1990er hörte und bis heute liebe, auf dem Klavier zu spielen. Parallel dazu ließ ich mich in Harmonielehre, Arrangement und Komposition ausbilden und hatte immer mehr Spaß am Musizieren. Ich lernte frei zu spielen. Jede Melodie, die ich hörte, produzierte ich problemlos nach. Synthesizer ermöglichten es uns, mit verschiedenen anderen Instrumenten außer Klavier und Schlagzeug zu musizieren.

Mit 17 Jahren komponierte ich meine ersten Stücke, ein Jahr später erschien mein Debüt-Album „My Dreams of Harmony". Ab 19 lernte ich E-Gitarre und Bass, beide Instrumente brachte ich mir selbst bei. Aktuell habe ich 8 E-Gitarren (Fender Telecaster) und einen Bass (Yamaha).

Mit der Zeit komponierte ich immer mehr. Waren es zuerst nur Instrumental-Songs, kamen dann immer mehr mit Texten (Lyrics) hinzu. Zuerst auf Deutsch, dann auf Englisch. Ich entwickelte eine Leidenschaft für Balladen und Pop Songs, aber mein Repertoire ist groß: Auch Rock, Blues, Jazz, Hip Hop, Swing, Heavy Metal, Funk, Schlager und andere Musikstile kann ich komponieren und spielen.

Zwischen 1998 und 2019 habe über 1200 Songs komponiert, von denen viele bereits auf CDs erschienen sind, andere noch veröffentlicht werden. Diese Buchreihe „WORKS" beinhaltet mein musikalisches Lebenswerk, die Texte aller Songs, die ich in den letzten 22 Jahren geschrieben habe. Das Zusammentragen hat mir viel Freude bereitet und die Lyrics bedeuten mir sehr viel.

Die Bücher Vol. 1 bis Vol. 3 beinhalten meine Lyrics aus dem Zeitraum 1998 bis 2013. Alles alphabetisch geordnet:
Vol. 1 = 1 - H
Vol. 2 = I - P
Vol. 3 = Q - Z

Vol. 4 bietet alle neuen Lyrics, die zwischen 2014 und 2019 entstanden sind. Und Vol. 5 präsentiert alle brandneuen Lyrics aus den Jahren 2019 und 2020.

Ich wünsche Ihnen viel Freude mit jenem Kompendium meiner musikalisch-lyrischen Arbeit!

Let´s Rock!
Abbas Schirmohammadi

1 - 9

15 YEARS FROM NOW

15 YEARS FROM NOW
I WANNA BE SUCH A STAR
STILL IN LOVE WITH ALL THE THINGS I DO
AND MY CAR
15 YEARS FROM NOW
ANOTHER MAN I WILL BE
THOUGH I´M OLDER THEN
I HOPE YOU ARE STILL WITH ME

15 YEARS FROM NOW
ANOTHER ONE, WE´LL BE 3
I WILL BUILD A HOUSE
WE´RE LIVING NOW BY THE SEA
15 YEARS FROM NOW
I DON´T LOOK BACK TO THE PAST
CAUSE THE TIMELINE FEEDS MY MEMORY
TO THE BEST

A MAGICAL LIGHT IS SHOWING ME HOME
WITH YOU AT MY SIDE I´M NEVER ALONE
I´M FIGHTING THE STONES, I´M FIGHTING THE LIES
THE POWER YOU GIVE, THE LOVE IN YOUR EYES

15 YEARS FROM NOW
DON´T KNOW THE TIME BUT I´M SURE
WORLD HAS CHANGED AROUND US ANYWHERE
I IGNORE
15 YEARS FROM NOW
OUR LOVE WILL BE JUST THE SAME
CAUSE WE STAND TOGETHER ALL THE TIME
SUN AND RAIN

A MAGICAL LIGHT IS SHOWING ME HOME
WITH YOU AT MY SIDE I´M NEVER ALONE
I´M FIGHTING THE STONES, I´M FIGHTING THE LIES
THE POWER YOU GIVE, THE LOVE IN YOUR EYES

5 TO 12 IN THE NIGHT

I´M SLEEPING IN MY LIVING ROOM FOR TONIGHT
THE PROBLEMS I JUST HAVE WITH YOU HIT THE LIGHT
ISN´T IT TRUE I FOUND
A MESSAGE OF SOMEONE ELSE?
AND I SAW A RIGHTFUL PICTURE OF HOLDING HANDS

YOU KNOW I´VE BEEN A LOVING ONE ALL MY LIFE
I´VE KISSED YOU QUITE SOME
HUNDRED TIMES EVERY NIGHT
NOW MY WORLD IS REALLY CHANGING NOW TO BE CLEAR
MAYBE I WILL PACK AND FINISH NOW BEING HERE

IT´S 5 TO 12 IN THE NIGHT
MY SHADOW IS WILLING TO GO
I TURN TO PUT ON THE LIGHT
YOU´RE WATCHING THE SHOW
THE LOVE IS STILL IN MY LIFE
THE COIN ISN´T READY TO FLY
THE SUNSHINE BATTLES THE KNIFE
I SEE YOU CRY

I´M EATING IN MY LIVING ROOM, TV´S ON
YOU´RE TRYING TO DECLARE YOURSELF ON AND ON
ISN´T IT TRUE I CRACKED A VIDEO MAKING LOVE?
DON´T YOU DARE TO SAY
YOU´RE NOT IN THIS SCENE OF LOVE

IT´S 5 TO 12 IN THE NIGHT
MY SHADOW IS WILLING TO GO
I TURN TO PUT ON THE LIGHT
YOU´RE WATCHING THE SHOW
THE LOVE IS STILL IN MY LIFE
THE COIN ISN´T READY TO FLY
THE SUNSHINE BATTLES THE KNIFE
I SEE YOU CRY

50 BUCKS

50 BUCKS
IS ALL I CANNOT GIVE RIGHT TO YOU
GOT NO WORK AND HAVE TO PAY THE RENT FOR ME TOO
IN MY WORLD I´M HERE FOR TENDERNESS
AND SOME LOVE
IF YOU LIKE MY STYLE JUST COME WITH ME
FOR SOME LOVE

50 BUCKS
IS ALL I HAVE IN MY UNWASHED HANDS
DON´T YOU DARE TO THINK OF ROBBING ME
LET´S BE FRIENDS
IN MY ROOM OF LOVE AND TENDERNESS, YOU AND I
WE´LL BE HAPPY WHILE THE WORLD OUTSIDE
MAKES ME DIE

SHOOTING A LIE
I AM READY TO STAY WITH YOU
MUTING MY CRY AS WE´RE DOING THE THINGS WE DO
WHISTLE ME LOVE IN A WORDING I UNDERSTAND
GIVE ME YOUR LOVE
TAKE MY HEARTBEAT INTO YOUR HANDS

1000 BUCKS I HAVE
I´M HAPPY NOW LIKE A KING
1000 BUCKS I HAD, A 400 PRETTY RING
THIS IS MORE YOU´VE EVER SEEN IN YOUR EMPTY LIFE
THIS IS MORE THAN I JUST EVER HAD IN MY LIFE

SHOOTING A LIE
I AM READY TO STAY WITH YOU
MUTING MY CRY AS WE´RE DOING THE THINGS WE DO
WHISTLE ME LOVE IN A WORDING I UNDERSTAND
GIVE ME YOUR LOVE
TAKE MY HEARTBEAT INTO YOUR HANDS

A - B

A DOOR TO THE LIGHT

I WANNA BE STRONG
QUITE MYSTERIOUS TIME
I KEEP HOLDING ON
DON´T TAKE ALL THE LINE

NEVER I THINK I WAS
FULL LIKE 2 ROOMS OF WINE
MAYBE I´M DOWN BECAUSE
I THOUGHT MY LIFE WAS FINE

STRONG I WAS BEFORE
STRONG I WAS ALRIGHT
SEARCHING FOR A DOOR
TO THE LIGHT
POWERS OF THE NIGHT
PAST AND NOW UNITE
HELP ME GETTING STRONG
GAINING MORE

I WANNA ESCAPE
DON´T GIVE UP ON ME
I OPEN THIS CAGE
ALL FREEDOM I SEE

STRONG I WAS BEFORE
STRONG I WAS ALRIGHT
SEARCHING FOR A DOOR
TO THE LIGHT
POWERS OF THE NIGHT
PAST AND NOW UNITE
HELP ME GETTING STRONG
GAINING MORE

A PLAIN AND SIMPLE LIE

AND THERE´S ANOTHER CORNER
ROUND THE LIVING OF THE NIGHT
I WANNA KNOW THE TRUTH BEHIND THE WALL
THERE´S SOMETHING DEEP INSIDE ME
I JUST WANNA SEE THE LIGHT
AND MAYBE I´M THE TOUGHEST TO THE FALL

I´M QUITE INTELLIGENT TO KNOW
THERE´S SOMETHING GOING ON
THE TRUTH IS ALWAYS FAR AWAY FROM US
I´M LOOKING FOR THE ANSWER
AND MY SEARCH IS GOING ON
I TAKE THE TRAIN AND DRIVE IN WITH THE BUS

A PLAIN AND SIMPLE ANSWER, A PLAIN AND SIMPLE LIE
THE TRUTH IS NEARLY FLYING AWAY
I KNOW THE WORLD IS TURNING, I KNOW I´M IN A MESS
THE NIGHT IS FALLING JUST TO BE THE DAY

THE POLITICS´ CORRUPTION
ISN´T STRONGER THAN BEFORE
BUT OBVIOUSLY IT´S GETTING EVEN MORE
THE MESSAGES WE GET
FROM ALL AROUND THIS CRAZY WORLD
ARE FIGHTING MEN AND LADIES, BOYS AND GIRLS

THERE´S JUST AN HANDFUL ALIEN
THAT RULE AND DOESN´T CARE
ESPECIALLY SINCE THAT DAY THEY CAME ALONG
THEY LOOK LIKE HUMAN MANKIND
BUT THEIR MIND IS SUCH A SCARE
YOU´RE CRAZY IF YOU THINK THEY RIGHT THE WRONG

A PLAIN AND SIMPLE ANSWER, A PLAIN AND SIMPLE LIE
THE TRUTH IS NEARLY FLYING AWAY
I KNOW THE WORLD IS TURNING, I KNOW I´M IN A MESS
THE NIGHT IS FALLING JUST TO BE THE DAY

A SIGN OF LOVE

A SIGN OF LOVE
I FOLLOW YOU
I UNDERSTAND
YOU LOVE ME TOO
THE MOMENT
OUR EYES BECAME
SO GOOD
I FEEL TO PLAY THIS GAME

I SEND YOU MESSAGES IN FLOWERS
I´M LOOKING FOR A DINNER DATE
HERE I AM WAITING FOR SOME HOURS
I FEEL YOU´RE REALLY KIND OF LATE

A SIGN OF LOVE
I UNDERSTAND
THIS WOMAN WANTS ME
AS HER FRIEND
FOR JUST 1 SECOND
OUR EYES
SAW WHAT IT IS
IT WILL BE NICE

I SEND YOU MESSAGES IN FLOWERS
I´M LOOKING FOR A DINNER DATE
HERE I AM WAITING FOR SOME HOURS
I FEEL YOU´RE REALLY KIND OF LATE

AS TIME IS PASSING BY
I THINK THE EYE CONTACT WAS REALLY NICE
HOT WILL BE OUR NIGHT
I´LL MAKE YOU HAPPY WITH A BIG SURPRISE

AN EASY LIFE

AN EASY LIFE I WANNA LIVE
NO ONE AROUND FOR ME TO WORRY
I NEED NO LOVE, I NEED NO PAIN
LEAVE ME ALONE AND TAKE THE TRAIN

I TRIED TO LIVE ALONG WITH YOU
IT WAS A TRY, IT WAS A NIGHTMARE
I COULDN´T SLEEP, I COULDN´T EAT
I HAD NO CHOICE BUT TO BE TRUE

AN EASY LIFE
AS TIME IS GOING BY
AN EASY LIFE
I DON´T NEED LOVE EVERY NIGHT
AN EASY LIFE
DISCUSSIONS BREAK MY HEART
AN EASY LIFE
I´M GONNA START HERE TONIGHT

I TRIED TO LOVE, I TRIED TO LIVE
ALONG WITH YOU AND FEEL THE SUNSHINE
I COULDN´T DO, I COULDN´T STAND
THIS WAY OF LIFE, NO HAPPY STAN

AN EASY LIFE
SO BETTER UNDERSTAND
AN EASY LIFE
I DON´T NEED YOU AS A FRIEND
AN EASY LIFE
SO I CAN SMILE AGAIN
AN EASY LIFE
YOU SEE A TRUE HAPPY MAN

ANOTHER LADY IN MY DAY

TAKE ME TO A PLACE
LIKE A BED OF ROSES
HERE I WANNA SLEEP
NOW WITH YOU

CANDLES IN THE WIND
MUSIC MAKES YOU HAPPY
AFTERWARDS I KNOW
IF IT´S TRUE

WHEN THIS NIGHT OF MAGIC TURNS AWAY
I WILL ASK MY HEART IF I SHOULD STAY
YOU CAN BE MY SUNSHINE IN THE RAIN
OR ANOTHER LADY IN MY DAY

I´M A LONELY ONE
LOOKING FOR A LADY
WILL I FIND THE ONE
OF MY HEART?

MAYBE YOU´RE THE ONE
IN THE BED OF ROSES
WE WILL SPEND 1 NIGHT
FOR THE START

WHEN THIS NIGHT OF MAGIC TURNS AWAY
I WILL ASK MY HEART IF I SHOULD STAY
YOU CAN BE MY SUNSHINE IN THE RAIN
OR ANOTHER LADY IN MY DAY

ANOTHER YEAR WITH YOU

MAYBE YOU CAN MAKE ME SMILE
MAYBE YOU WILL MAKE ME FLY
ARE YOU THE LADY
I´VE NOT SEEN BEFORE?
ARE YOU THE SUNSHINE
COMING THROUGH MY DOOR?

MAYBE YOU CAN MAKE ME CRY
MAYBE YOU WILL STEAL AND LIE
ARE YOU THE LADY
BREAKING ME APART?
ARE YOU A DEMON
POISONING MY HEART?

THOUGH YOUR EYES ARE SHINING
I DON´T KNOW IF YOU´RE TRUE
GIVE ME JUST ANOTHER YEAR WITH YOU
IF YOU´RE FREAKIN´ CRAZY
AND IF YOUR LOVE IS WRONG
I JUST NEED A CHANCE TO CARRY ON

MAYBE YOU WILL BE MY WIFE
MAYBE YOU KEEP ME ALIVE
I MAY BE WRONG
IF YOU HAVE OTHER PLANS
A CRUEL DESTRUCTION
BUT A SEXY CHANCE

LOVE IT WHEN YOU KISS ME
AND MISS YOU WHEN YOU´RE GONE
I JUST NEED A CHANCE TO CARRY ON
LOVE IT WHEN YOU TOUCH ME
ANOTHER RENDEZVOUS
GIVE ME JUST ANOTHER YEAR WITH YOU

APPLE-MELON PIE

MY EMPTY STOMACH SCREAMS FOR FOOD TONIGHT
AROUND THIS CORNER I CAN SMELL
AN APPLE-MELON PIE
AND I NEED TO TAKE IT AWAY
THE SWEET JUST MAKES ME HIGH
IN MY DAY

DUCK TALES
CENT OF MAGIC IN MY ROOM
I EAT APPLE-MELON PIE
MY MOOD IS CHANGING
TO SOME BETTER NOW
THE SWEET JUST MAKES ME FLY
ANOTHER PIE

DON´T LIKE THIS PAIN I HAVE FROM DRINKING JUST
WHEN THERE´S NO POWER IN MY BRAIN
AN APPLE-MELON PIE
MAKES ME HAPPY DAY AND ALL NIGHT
I SWEAR YOU´RE OUT OF LIE
TO BE TRUE

DUCK TALES
CENT OF MAGIC IN MY ROOM
I EAT APPLE-MELON PIE
MY MOOD IS CHANGING
TO SOME BETTER NOW
THE SWEET JUST MAKES ME FLY
ANOTHER PIE

ARE YOU A FRIEND?

ARE YOU A FRIEND WHEN I JUST NEED YOUR HELP?
GIVE ME YOUR HAND AND HELP ME UP, MY FRIEND
I NEVER THOUGHT OF THIS
I NEVER SAW MY LIFE
COULD BE IN DANGER NOW
I NEED TO STAY ALIVE

ARE YOU A FRIEND? MAYBE IT´S ALL IN YOU
MONEY I NEED, MONEY IS GONE, IT´S TRUE
I HAD A MILLION BUCKS
A WEALTHY STATE OF LIFE
BUT SOMEHOW LOST IN SPACE
I NEED TO STAY ALIVE

IS IT A DREAM? IS IT REALITY?
I´M LOSING MY STATE OF LIFE
TURNING THE TIME BACK TO PARADISE DAYS
I´M LOSING THE GRIP OF TIME
ARE YOU A FRIEND OR A PIG IN THE NIGHT?
THE TRUTH ISN´T FAR AWAY
HELP ME OR GO
BIG DECISIONS ARE MADE TODAY

ARE YOU A FRIEND WHEN I LOOK OUT FOR MORE?
I´M NOW IN NEED, OPEN OR CLOSE YOUR DOOR
BUT IF YOU TURN AWAY
AND IF I STAY ALIVE
I´M GONNA COME BACK STRONG
AND RUIN YOUR WEALTHY LIFE

IS IT A DREAM? IS IT REALITY?
I´M LOSING MY STATE OF LIFE
TURNING THE TIME BACK TO PARADISE DAYS
I´M LOSING THE GRIP OF TIME
ARE YOU A FRIEND OR A PIG IN THE NIGHT?
THE TRUTH ISN´T FAR AWAY
HELP ME OR GO
BIG DECISIONS ARE MADE TODAY

ARE YOU AN ALIEN?

MAKING LOVE IN DIFFERENT ROOMS
THE FUTURE NOW HAS COME
YOU AND I ARE HAVING SO MUCH FUN
KISSING OTHER PEOPLE
NEVER EVER IN MY LIFE
THOUGH IT´S VERY DIFFERENT WE´RE ALIVE

ARE YOU AN ALIEN?
ARE YOU AN ALIEN?
EVERYBODY LIVES ALONE
JUST LIKE AN ALIEN
ARE YOU AN ALIEN?
PRISONED IN A WORLD OF HOME
MAKING LOVE
IN DIFFERENT BEDROOMS IN THE NIGHT
HIGH ABOVE
I THINK THE ALIEN IS RIGHT

MAKING LOVE IN DIFFERENT ROOMS
AND BEAMING IT TO YOU
WATCHING HOW YOU DO IT EVERY NIGHT
MAYBE IT´S A KISS I MISS
I´M MISSING ALL OF YOU
MAKING LOVE IN DIFFERENT KINDS OF LIGHT

ARE YOU AN ALIEN?
ARE YOU AN ALIEN?
EVERYBODY LIVES ALONE
JUST LIKE AN ALIEN
ARE YOU AN ALIEN?
PRISONED IN A WORLD OF HOME
MAKING LOVE
IN DIFFERENT BEDROOMS IN THE NIGHT
HIGH ABOVE
I THINK THE ALIEN IS RIGHT

ARE YOU DISAPPOINTED TOO?

YOU´RE ON ANOTHER ROAD
DRIVING FAR AWAY
I THOUGHT WE´RE GETTING OLD
LIKE A PAIR THEY SAY

I KNEW WE HAD A CHANCE
SAW IT IN YOUR EYES
I TOOK YOU OUT TO DANCE
MAN, I FELT ALIVE

ARE YOU DISAPPOINTED TOO?
I HAD PLANS TO MARRY YOU
NEVER WILL I UNDERSTAND
WHY YOU TOOK ANOTHER MAN

SWEET VOICES IN MY HEAD
I WILL LOSE MY MIND
I THINK OF WHAT YOU SAID
MAYBE I WAS BLIND

LOVE WAS ANOTHER HIGH
AS THE GOOD OL´ KISS
YOU MADE ME FEEL SO HIGH
ALL OF YOU I MISS

ARE YOU DISAPPOINTED TOO?
I HAD PLANS TO MARRY YOU
NEVER WILL I UNDERSTAND
WHY YOU TOOK ANOTHER MAN

I START TO CRY
WHERE SHALL I GO?
I DON´T SEE NO SENSE ANYMORE
MAYBE SOME DAY
MAYBE SOME TIME
YOU´LL COME BACK AND MAKE ME FEEL FINE

ASBURY PARK

TOBACCO ROAD, THE CITY FAR BEHIND
I´M ON MY WAY TO FREEDOM NOW I FIND
SOME 20 YEARS I DID IT ALL
SOME 20 MORE AND I WILL FALL

ASBURY PARK, NEW JERSEY, I´M ALIVE
I´M COMING HOME TO FIND ANOTHER LIFE
I LEFT BEHIND STUPIDITY
I WANNA FIND A CHANCE FOR ME

SOME STUPID 20 YEARS OF LIFE
NOT 1 MORE DAY
I NEARLY MISSED THE CUE
TO GET UP ANYWAY
I LEFT BEHIND THE JOB I DID
I DID IT GOOD
I NEVER THOUGHT I HAD THE GUTS TO GO
I COULD

ASBURY PARK, SOME MEMORIES IN MY MIND
I WENT TO SCHOOL AND STUDIED GIRLS AND WINE
I NEVER THOUGHT I´D LEAVE THIS PLACE
I FOUND A JOB QUITE OUT OF SPACE

SOME STUPID 20 YEARS OF LIFE
NOT 1 MORE DAY
I NEARLY MISSED THE CUE
TO GET UP ANYWAY
I LEFT BEHIND THE JOB I DID
I DID IT GOOD
I NEVER THOUGHT I HAD THE GUTS TO GO
I COULD

AT THE BEACH OF SANSIBAR

WHISKY DRINKING, SMOKING CIGARETTES
AND DANCING TO THE MUSIC BOX
WATCHING ALL THE GIRLS AND ALL THE LADIES
DANCING TO ANNIE LENNOX
AT THE BEACH OF SANSIBAR
I´M OPEN FOR A NIGHT OF JOY AND FUN
WHISKY DRINKING, SMOKING CIGARETTES
AND HAVING SEX BEFORE I´M GONE

WITH LADY LUCK JUST BY MY SIDE
I FIND THE PRETTIEST ONE OF ALL TO TAKE A RIDE
DON´T SPEND SOME MONEY FOR A THING
I JUST CAN HAVE WITHOUT HER BUYING ANY RING
I TAKE A BLONDE OF 21
I TAKE HER SISTER TOO WITH 18 YEARS OF FUN
WE´LL HAVE A NIGHT I WON´T FORGET
NEXT NIGHT I´LL WAKE UP ONLY LONELY IN MY BED

TURNING ON THE VIDEO
I WANNA KEEP THIS MOMENT IN MY MIND
WATCHING ALL THE GIRLS IN ACTION
MAKE ME HAPPY IN THE MORNING LIGHT
ANNABELLE, MY QUEEN OF LOVE
AND LYDIA, YOU´RE BLOWING UP MY BRAIN
GOT IT ALL ON VIDEO
I´M WATCHING AS THEY´RE DRIVING ME INSANE

WITH LADY LUCK JUST BY MY SIDE
I FOUND THE PRETTIEST ONE OF ALL TO TAKE A RIDE
DON´T SPEND SOME MONEY FOR A THING
I JUST CAN HAVE WITHOUT HER BUYING ANY RING
I TOOK A BLONDE OF 21
I TOOK HER SISTER TOO WITH 18 YEARS OF FUN
WE HAD A NIGHT I WON´T FORGET
THIS NIGHT I WOKE UP ONLY LONELY IN MY BED

BARON CORBIN DAY

THE SILENCE THAT I HAD
IN MY HEAD
THE DEMONS ALL I SAW
ROUND MY BED

I NEVER THOUGHT
THIS WORLD GETS CRAZY IN A DAY
I NEVER DREAMT OF GOING NOWHERE
LOST MY WAY

LISTEN TO ME, ALL THE LOVERS IN THE NIGHT
BARON CORBIN DAY
THINGS ARE HAPPENING TONIGHT
DON´T YOU REPEAT
DON´T YOU DARE TO STEAL THE LIGHT
HEY, ARE YOU READY FOR A FIGHT?

THE SADNESS OF MY HEART
SLOWED ME DOWN
SO BROKEN WAS THE GLASS
ALL AROUND

THE WORLD IS CHANGING NOW
TO MAYBE BETTER TIMES
AND WHEN THE SUN IS TAKING OVER
MY LIFE SHINES

LISTEN TO ME, ALL THE LOVERS IN THE NIGHT
BARON CORBIN DAY
THINGS ARE HAPPENING TONIGHT
DON´T YOU REPEAT
DON´T YOU DARE TO STEAL THE LIGHT
HEY, ARE YOU READY FOR A FIGHT?

BE MY GOLD

A TRUTH I DON´T LIKE
IS A TRUTH I DON´T WANNA BELIEVE
THOUGH MUSTAFA TOLD ME A STORY
THAT YOU WANNA LEAVE
I´VE NEVER BEEN PRETTY
I´VE NEVER BEEN RICH IN MY LIFE
BUT ONE THING I KNOW IS
MY LOVE FOR YOU KEEPS ME ALIVE

GLORIOUS TIME WILL BE OVER YOU TAKE IT AWAY
TRUTH VERSUS LIE
WILL YOU LEAVE MY LIFE OR WILL YOU STAY?
BURNING THE BRIDGES AWAY

PUZZLING UP IN MY HEAD TONIGHT
IF YOU LEAVE ME FOR SURE AND AWAY
THINKING OF WHAT IT IS TONIGHT
BETTER SHOW ME YOUR LOVE NIGHT AND DAY
WAITING NOW FOR YOUR WORD OF GOLD
PRAYING NOW YOU STILL BE MY GOLD

A LIE I DON´T LIKE IS A LIE I DON´T WANNA TAKE CARE
AND MAYBE THE THINGS
THAT OLD MUSTAFA TOLD ME AIN´T THERE
I´VE NEVER BEEN SMOKING
I´VE NEVER BEEN DRINKING MY TIME
WAS HAPPY WITH YOU
AND SO LUCKY I KNEW YOU WERE MINE

TELL ME THE TRUTH, IS IT OVER AND IS IT FOR SURE?
WAITING FOR YOU
IS THERE SOMEONE AND CALLING MY DOOR?
NEVER AGAIN AND BEFORE

PUZZLING UP IN MY HEAD TONIGHT
IF YOU LEAVE ME FOR SURE AND AWAY
THINKING OF WHAT IT IS TONIGHT
BETTER SHOW ME YOUR LOVE NIGHT AND DAY
WAITING NOW FOR YOUR WORD OF GOLD
PRAYING NOW YOU STILL BE MY GOLD

BEST IN LIFE

MAYBE I DIDN´T READ YOUR RHYMIN´ WORDS
MAYBE I DIDN´T SEE YOUR POINTED SKIRT
NEVER FOUND SOME TIME TO STAY WITH YOU
DIDN´T KNOW ABOUT YOUR LIFE
NEVER THOUGHT I´D BE IN LOVE WITH YOU
NOW TONIGHT

MAYBE YOU DIDN´T TRY TO COME TOO CLOSE
MAYBE YOU THOUGHT YOU SHOULDN´T TAKE ME HOME
DIDN´T KNOW YOU WERE IN LOVE WITH ME
DIDN´T THINK I HAD A CHANCE
IN MY DEEPEST DARKEST FANTASY
HOLDING HANDS

SO BETTER OPEN YOUR EYES
OR THE MAGIC GETS KILLED BY LIES
THE STARS ARE REACHABLE THOUGH
IF YOU DON´T LET THEM GO
JUST GRAB THE LIGHT
DON´T LOOK AWAY, DON´T RUN AWAY
OR YOU WILL LOSE THE BEST IF LIFE

MAYBE I WAS INFECTED TO BE TRUE
MAYBE YOUR HEART ELECTED ME AND YOU
NEVER THOUGHT MY LIFE COULD BETTER BE
WITH A GIRL LIKE YOU BEFORE
AS WE HEAD UP TO THE SUN AGAIN
OUT FOR MORE

SO BETTER OPEN YOUR EYES
OR THE MAGIC GETS KILLED BY LIES
THE STARS ARE REACHABLE THOUGH
IF YOU DON´T LET THEM GO
JUST GRAB THE LIGHT
DON´T LOOK AWAY, DON´T RUN AWAY
OR YOU WILL LOSE THE BEST OF LIFE

BITTER LOVE

I HAVE JUST DIED
MY SOUL IS MOVING ON
HOLDING ME CLOSE
IN TEARS TO RIGHT A WRONG
I´M LOOKING DOWN AT YOU
SHOOTING STAR

END OF MY LIFE
THE DOCTOR SHOOK HIS HEAD
END OF MY TIME
WAS DYING IN THIS BED
MY BODY´S GETTING COLD
COMES THE CAR

BITTER LOVE IS IN YOUR EYES
AS YOU SAY GOODBYE AS I WAVE GOODBYE
HIDE YOUR TEARS AND STAY ALIVE
AND ENJOY YOUR TIME AND ENJOY YOUR LIFE

FLYING AWAY
THE LIGHT IS COMING CLOSE
LIGHTER I FEEL
JUST LIKE AN OVERDOSE
I FEEL I´M GOIN´ YOUNG
ONCE AGAIN

SUNSHINE I SEE
THIS GOLDEN PLACE IS MINE
LOOKIN´ ON DOWN
I SEE YOU SCREAM AND CRY
BE SURE YOU´LL FIND SOME LOVE
ONCE AGAIN

BITTER LOVE IS IN YOUR EYES
AS YOU SAY GOODBYE AS I WAVE GOODBYE
HIDE YOUR TEARS AND STAY ALIVE
AND ENJOY YOUR TIME AND ENJOY YOUR LIFE

BLACK OR WHITE

HOT, THE SUN IS SHINING DOWN
HEAT, NO WORKING GIRLS AROUND
BEACH, GET READY, HERE I COME
FRIENDS, WE´RE HAVING SO MUCH FUN

AS I DIVE INTO THE SEA
THERE´S A SHADOW AFTER ME

I DON´T KNOW IF SHE´S BLACK OR WHITE
A BLONDE ONE OR A SKINNY GIRL
I FEEL HER BODY TOUCHING
MY LUSTFUL WORLD
WELL, MAYBE SHE´S AMERICAN
A SWEDISH OR A RUSSIAN QUEEN
AS SOON AS I GET UP AGAIN
I WILL SEE

STARS ARE WHIRLING IN MY BRAIN
STILL DON´T KNOW ABOUT HER NAME
SOON I´LL SEE HER SHINY FACE
THEN WE´LL START THE LOVING CHASE

AS I DIVE INTO THE BLUE
I CAN FEEL THE LOVE OF YOU

I DON´T KNOW IF YOU´RE BLACK OR WHITE
A BLONDE ONE OR A SKINNY GIRL
I FEEL YOUR BODY TOUCHING
MY LUSTFUL WORLD
WELL, MAYBE YOU´RE AMERICAN
A SWEDISH OR A RUSSIAN QUEEN
AS SOON AS I GET UP AGAIN
I WILL SEE

BLUE-EYED RED-LIPPED LADY

BLUE-EYED LADY
WITH A SECRET SMILE
I´M INTERESTED IN YOU
RED-LIPPED BABY
WITH A SPECIAL STYLE
THIS IS SOMETHING WE CAN DO

MY BED IS EMPTY LIKE
A GLASS OF WATER LIKE
WITH JUST 1 DRINK FOR YOU

BLUE-EYED LADY ON AGAIN
SHOW ME LOVE AND KISS YOUR MAN
RED-LIPPED BABY, I´M WITH YOU
DREAMIN´ DREAMS OF LOVIN´ YOU

WHEN I SAW YOU
AT THE SWIMMING POOL
LYING, FEELING THE SUN
DID MY BUSINESS
IN A CHANGING ROOM
THINGS WERE REALLY SAID AND DONE

MY HEART IS FULL OF YOU
AND SO I STEP INTO
YOUR LIFE AND TAKE YOU HOME

BLUE-EYED LADY ON AGAIN
SHOW ME LOVE AND KISS YOUR MAN
RED-LIPPED BABY, I´M WITH YOU
DREAMIN´ DREAMS OF LOVIN´ YOU

BOW DOWN TO THE KING

IS IT REALLY TRUE THEY CALL ME LARGER THAN LIFE?
IF IT´S TRUE I´M HERE NOW TO STAY
COMING FROM A DIFFERENT WORLD
I´M BETTER THAN YOU
NOW I´M HERE AND I WON´T GO AWAY

IS IT REALLY TRUE THEY CALL ME MASTER OF MIND?
IF IT´S TRUE I´M MASTER OF GAMES
DOIN´ WHAT I WANT AND TAKE ADVANTAGE OF YOU
SHOWING YOU THE POWER OF THE FLAMES

BOW DOWN TO THE KING, I´M KING OF EVERYTHING
SORROW I LEAVE BEHIND
BOW DOWN TO THE KING, I´M MISTER DING-A-LING
GOLD IS THE LAND FOR ME, THEY ARE TOO BLIND TO SEE

IS IT REALLY TRUE THEY CALL ME LIGHT OF THE STARS?
IF IT´S TRUE I KNOW HOW TO SHINE
STANDING RIGHT ON TOP AND LET THEM CARRY A HOUSE
TO THE PLACE I KNOW I´M FEELING FINE

COMING FROM A DIFFERENT WORLD
THEY REALLY BELIEVE
SORRY, GIRLS AND GUYS, I´M FROM SPAIN
WON´T YOU TELL YOU THAT
CAUSE YOU BELIEVE IN THE STARS
SO I´M GONNA PLAY WITH YOU THIS GAME

BOW DOWN TO THE KING, I´M KING OF EVERYTHING
SORROW I LEAVE BEHIND
BOW DOWN TO THE KING, I´M MISTER DING-A-LING
GOLD IS THE LAND FOR ME, THEY ARE TOO BLIND TO SEE

RIGHT HERE ON TIME
THIS LAND IS MINE
I´M LARGER THAN MY SHADY LIFE
HAIL TO YOUR KING
SPREADING MY WINGS
I RULE THIS LAND UNTIL I DIE

C - F

CALL ME MR. WHITTAKER

CALL ME MR. WHITTAKER ALTHOUGH THAT´S NOT MY NAME
I´VE COME TO SPEND A LOT OF MONEY
IF YOU WANNA PLAY MY GAME
SO CLOSE THE DOOR AND TURN AROUND THE KEY
AND SHOW ME WHAT YOU GOT
I´M GONNA TELL YOU WHAT I WANT FROM YOU
WE´RE GONNA HAVE IT HOT

TAKE A SHOWER NOW WITH ME AND LEAD ME TO THE POOL
IN WHICH WE START THE LOVING GAME
YOU HAVE TO FOLLOW EVERY RULE
MY STIPULATIONS ARE OUTSTANDING
AND MY WISHES TURN YOU ON
WE´RE GONNA HAVE A LOT OF FUN TOGETHER
TIL THE MORNING SUN

THUNDER AND SOME LIGHTNING
TEASING AND SOME BITING
LEATHERFACE WAXING ME AWAY
PUNCHES AND SOME SCREAMING
MAKE A HAPPY FEELING
PAYING ALL FOR A BETTER DAY

CALL ME MR. WHITTAKER AS I CALL YOU JACQUELINE
I´M VERY PROUD OF HOW YOU DID THE THINGS
THE DIRTY AND THE MEAN
MY LIST IS ENDLESS AND I´M PAYING FOR
GOOD BUSINESS ISN´T CHEAP
AND SO WE´RE MOVING ON TO HIMMELBETT
YOU´RE GONNA GET IT DEEP

TAKE ANOTHER LOAD AND MAKE ANOTHER OUT OF ME
BEFORE I GO I´LL LET YOU KNOW
IF YOU FULFILLED MY FANTASY
AND MAYBE EXTRA GOOD IS 50 PLUS
SO GIVE YOUR VERY BEST, JACQUELINE
YOU´RE QUITE OUTSTANDING, I MUST SAY
MY MONEY ON YOUR CHEST

THUNDER AND SOME LIGHTNING
TEASING AND SOME BITING
LEATHERFACE WAXING ME AWAY
PUNCHES AND SOME SCREAMING
MAKE A HAPPY FEELING
PAYING ALL FOR A BETTER DAY

CHANCE OF CERTAIN WAYS

I NEED TO KNOW WHAT IS WRONG WITH YOU
SOME ANSWERS I WANT TO HEAR
BETRAYING IS ONE BUT HIDING TWO
COME OUT IF YOU´RE SOMEWHERE HERE
THE STORY IS SUCH A SIMPLE ONE
I GAVE YOU A DOLLAR-LIFE
THE MONEY AND LOVE I SHARED WITH YOU
MADE YOU HAPPY AS MY WIFE

REMEMBER THE DAY I MARRIED YOU
YOU SWORE BY THE STARS ABOVE
FOREVER YOU´LL BE MY SUPERGIRL
AND GIVE ME ALL YOUR LOVE
I WORKED FOR 2 AND I WORKED FOR YOU
WHILE YOU JUST ENJOYED YOUR TIME
THE PROBLEM IS WITH ANOTHER ONE
YOU ARE HAVING A GOOD TIME

I WANNA EAT AND KICK HIS FACE
IS THERE ANOTHER ONE?
I JUST NEED TO KNOW WHAT´S GOING ON
YOU HAD THE CHANCE OF CERTAIN WAYS
YOU BETTER GO TONIGHT
OR I´LL KICK YOU OUT INTO THE NIGHT

AND NOW IT IS OVER, TAKE YOUR CLOTHES
I TURN AWAY FOR GOODBYE
THE GOLDEN RING ON YOUR HAND IS MINE
AND FINALLY NOW YOU CRY
YOU´RE ASKING ME FOR A SECOND CHANCE
BUT „STUPID“ IS NOT MY NAME
I TURN AROUND, CLOSE THE DOOR FOR SURE
LEAVE YOU CRYING IN THE RAIN

I WANNA EAT AND KICK HIS FACE
IS THERE ANOTHER ONE?
I JUST NEED TO KNOW WHAT´S GOING ON
YOU HAD THE CHANCE OF CERTAIN WAYS
YOU BETTER GO TONIGHT
OR I´LL KICK YOU OUT INTO THE NIGHT

CHOCOLATE CHIPS

SHOW YOU PICTURES OF MY HEAVY LIFE
MAKING ME FEEL ALIVE
SINCE MY BIRTH I´M REALLY IN A MESS
CHOCOLATE CHIPS, I MUST CONFESS

DAD WAS CRUEL AND MUMMY WENT AWAY
BUT I JUST HAD TO STAY
NOW I´M DOUBLE-DECKER ANYWAY
EATING MY LIFE AWAY

OH MAN, THE CHOCOLATE CHIPS ARE BURNING
CAN I BEHOLD INSTEAD OF TURNING?
LIFE CAN BE SUNSHINE, CHOCOLATE LADY
I´M SO ADDICTED TO YOU, BABY

NOW I´M FEELING LITTLE LITTLE LOW
CAUSE I JUST CANNOT GO
FEED ME, SPEED ME, HEAVY IS MY LIFE
CHIPS OF CHOCOLATE MAKE ME HIGH

I CAN TELL YOU NEVER IN A DAY
WILL I PUT FOOD AWAY
IF YOU THINK I´M MESSING UP MY LIFE
BABY, I´M SO ALIVE!

OH MAN, THE CHOCOLATE CHIPS ARE BURNING
CAN I BEHOLD INSTEAD OF TURNING?
LIFE CAN BE SUNSHINE, CHOCOLATE LADY
I´M SO ADDICTED TO YOU, BABY

CLIMBING UP THE LADDER

HEY, WHAT´S GOIN´ ON?
WHAT´S GOIN´ ON? WHAT´S GOIN´ ON?
HEY, WHAT´S GOIN´ ON?
WHAT´S GOIN´ ON? WHAT´S GOIN´ ON?

PICKING UP THE LADDER AND I WONDER WHERE I GO
FOLLOWING THE LADDER TO A PLACE I´VE SEEN BEFORE
WHERE AM I AND WHO AM I?
I WONDER WHAT WILL BE
FOLLOWING THIS LADDER
TO A PLACE I HAVE TO BE

INTO A SEA OF LOVE I DIVE
UP TO A SECRET PLACE I FLY
NEAR TO THE RAINBOW I WILL GO
ON TO ANOTHER PRETTY SHOW

HEY, WHAT´S GOIN´ ON?
WHAT´S GOIN´ ON? WHAT´S GOIN´ ON?
HEY, WHAT´S GOIN´ ON?
WHAT´S GOIN´ ON? WHAT´S GOIN´ ON?

MOVING UP THE LADDER
CLIMBING HIGHER THAN BEFORE
FOLLOWING THE LADDER TO A PLACE I´VE BEEN BEFORE
LIGHT INTO THE DARKNESS
AND THEN DARKNESS INTO LIGHT
FOLLOWING THE LADDER TO A PLACE I FEEL ALRIGHT

INTO A SEA OF LOVE I DIVE
UP TO A SECRET PLACE I FLY
NEAR TO THE RAINBOW I WILL GO
ON TO ANOTHER PRETTY SHOW

CLIMBING UP THE LADDER TO ESCAPE MY SHADY LIFE
HONESTLY THIS LADDER MAKES ME HAPPY AND ALIVE
MOVING TO ANOTHER PLACE
WHERE TIME IS STANDING STILL
FOLLOWING THE WAY TO WHERE
I CAN RELAX AND CHILL

CONFESSIONS OF LOVE

WHEN THE NIGHT COMES AGAIN
LIKE A PEDIGREE
WHEN THE DAWN IN MY EYES
BREAKS ME DOWN

IS IT A DREAM I NEVER GET OUT?
I COULD CRY ANOTHER AGAIN
IS IT REAL
OR IS IT A DREAM?

CONFESSIONS OF LOVE AND A KISS
IS IT OVER NOW?
IT´S A TURNAROUND
I NEVER GET CLOSER LIKE THIS
I CAN RUN AWAY
I CAN TEND TO STAY

THERE IS LOVE IN YOUR EYES
YOU´RE MY SUPERGIRL
HIGH ABOVE ENDLESS LOVE
IT´S MY DAY

IS IT A NIGHT WITH TEARS AND WITH JOY?
IF I CRY I GET UP AND SMILE
AS MY WORLD
IS CHANGING AGAIN

CONFESSIONS OF LOVE AND A KISS
IS IT OVER NOW?
IT´S A TURNAROUND
I NEVER GET CLOSER LIKE THIS
I CAN RUN AWAY
I CAN TEND TO STAY

CREEPY NIGHTMARE

AS THIS PLANE
IS CRASHING DOWN ON ME
I CAN´T BREATH
JUST WOODY CLOUDS I SEE
LIKE A BOMB
THE TREES ARE BREAKING DOWN
BREAKING BONES
THERE´S NO ONE ELSE AROUND

BIG AND BLACK
THE PLANE WAS GOING TO
SOMEWHERE I
WOULD SPEND THE NIGHT WITH YOU
NOW I´M BRUISED
AND NEARLY DEAD YOU SEE
PLANS DID CHANCE
BIG PLANE FELL DOWN ON ME

PLANE WRECK, A SCENE CHECK
HOT SMOKE IN THE AIR
MY LIFE´S A CREEPY NIGHTMARE
I WAS A SOLDIER, SO COLD NOW I FEEL
MAYBE I WILL DIE DOWN HERE

ALL THE PEOPLE
IN THIS PLANE HAVE DIED
CAPTAIN, STEWARDESSES
LOST THEIR FIGHT
WHY ON EARTH
IS GOD SO CRUEL? I CRY
SOON I´LL SEE
MY BUDDIES IN THE SKY

PLANE WRECK, A SCENE CHECK
HOT SMOKE IN THE AIR
MY LIFE´S A CREEPY NIGHTMARE
I WAS A SOLDIER, SO COLD NOW I FEEL
MAYBE I WILL DIE DOWN HERE

CURLY WURLY

HOLD YOU IN THE NIGHT UNTIL THE MORNING
CURLY WURLY IS YOUR HAIR UP ON MY CHEST
NAKED LIKE A GLASS WITHOUT SOME WATER
IN MY ARMS YOU DREAM A DREAM OF ALL THE BEST

HOLY TIME
AS THE MINUTES OF THE DAY ARE PASSING BY
I WANNA GO
WHERE IS NOW?
AS THE TIME IS RUNNING FAST I´M SLEEPING SLOW
I WANNA GO

YOUR CURLY WURLY DREAM OF LOVE
OUT OF 10 I REALLY FLY UP TO YOU
A SCENE OF MAGIC´S GOING BY
AS MY CAULIFLOWER LIFE IS UP TO YOU
NOW 1 BUT 2

LOVE YOU IN THE NIGHT LIKE THERE´S NO MORNING
QUITE HORRENDOUS IS THE PAIN JUST IN MY HEAD
MAYBE ALL THE TIME I WAS A LONER
LOOKING FORWARD WITH THIS ANGEL IN MY BED

YOU AND I
FOUND TOGETHER LIKE A FLY INTO THE LIGHT
I WANNA GO
HOLD ME TIGHT
AS THE NEXT NIGHT OF THE DAY IS PASSING BY
I WANNA GO

YOUR CURLY WURLY DREAM OF LOVE
OUT OF 10 I REALLY FLY UP TO YOU
A SCENE OF MAGIC´S GOING BY
AS MY CAULIFLOWER LIFE IS UP TO YOU
NOW 1 BUT 2

DANGEROUS GAMES

I LEAVE YOU AND GO TO ANOTHER I LIKE
SPENDING MY TIME WITH A GIN TONIGHT
BETTER NOW I FEEL AND TO ANOTHER HOUSE I GO
SHE´S A DIFFERENT ONE AND GOOD I KNOW
NEVER IN A DAY AND NEVER IN A NIGHT
WILL I BE NO´D BY MY SECOND TRY
NEVER IN A DAY AND NEVER IN A NIGHT
WILL I BE NO´D BY MY SECOND TRY

DANGEROUS GAMES I DON´T WANNA PLAY
WANNA HAVE FUN TONIGHT
LOSING MY FIRST, NOT MY SECOND CHANCE
THIS TIME I´LL MAKE IT RIGHT
DANGEROUS GAMES I JUST LIGHTEN UP
REGGAEING ON MY GUITAR
FINALLY FOUND I WAS LOOKING FOR
YOU ARE MY SHOOTING STAR

I LEAVE YOU AND GO CAUSE IT´S SOMETHING ROUND 8
ENDING THIS REAL SATISFYING DATE
GOTTA GET TO WORK WITHOUT A DINNER OR A DATE
LOOKING FORWARD TO THE BELL OF 8
NEVER IN A DAY AND NEVER IN A NIGHT
WILL I BE NO´D BY MY SECOND TRY
NEVER IN A DAY AND NEVER IN A NIGHT
WILL I BE NO´D BY MY SECOND TRY

DANGEROUS GAMES I DON´T WANNA PLAY
WANNA HAVE FUN TONIGHT
LOSING MY FIRST, NOT MY SECOND CHANCE
THIS TIME I´LL MAKE IT RIGHT
DANGEROUS GAMES I JUST LIGHTEN UP
REGGAEING ON MY GUITAR
FINALLY FOUND I WAS LOOKING FOR
YOU ARE MY SHOOTING STAR

I LOVE YOU AND GO TO VACATION I LIKE
SPENDING MY TIME WITH A GIN TONIGHT
BETTER NOW I FEEL, I SEE ANOTHER SEXY SHOW
SHE´S A PRETTY ONE AND GOOD I KNOW
NEVER IN A DAY AND NEVER IN A NIGHT
WILL I BE NO´D BY MY SECOND TRY
NEVER IN A DAY AND NEVER IN A NIGHT
WILL I BE NO´D BY MY SECOND TRY

DEAD AS YOU ARE

DEAD AS YOU ARE
I DON´T WANNA SLEEP WITH YOU
THERE´S NO POWER LEFT INSIDE OF YOU
DEAD AS YOU FEEL
AFTER JUST 1 WORKING DAY
I CAN´T SEE THIS SHAME AND DRIVE AWAY

DEAD AS YOU ARE
I DON´T WANNA HOLD YOU CLOSE
SEEMS YOU LOST YOUR LIFE TO OVERDOSE
DEAD AS YOU FEEL
EVERY DAY I´M COMING HOME
I GET OUT AND LEAVE, I´M ALL ALONE

I PRAY FOR YOU
MAYBE YOU GET YOUR POWERS BACK
I CRY FOR YOU
SORROW AND PAIN I FEEL
THINKING OF YOU
ALL OF THE GOLDEN MEMORIES
YOU WERE MY QUEEN
GIVING ME LOVE AND LIGHT

DEAD AS YOU ARE
I DON´T WANNA SPEND MY TIME
NO, I DON´T FEEL FINE TO BE WITH YOU
DEAD AS YOU FEEL
WANNA VIDEO YOUR EYES
SHOW YOU WHAT I SEE AND PAY THE PRICE

I PRAY FOR YOU
MAYBE YOU GET YOUR POWERS BACK
I CRY FOR YOU
SORROW AND PAIN I FEEL
THINKING OF YOU
ALL OF THE GOLDEN MEMORIES
YOU WERE MY QUEEN
GIVING ME LOVE AND LIGHT

DER SEEMANN IN DER HÜTTE

DER SEEMANN IN DER HÜTTE IST ALLEIN
VON ALL DEN KÄMPFEN HAT ER EIN HOLZBEIN
ER SCHLUG DIE SCHLIMMSTEN SEERÄUBER IN FLUCHT
SEIN SCHIFF LIEGT IMMER STARTKLAR IN DER BUCHT

DER SEEMANN IN DER HÜTTE LÄDT DICH EIN
IHR HISST DIE SEGEL, HOLT DEN ANKER EIN
DER PAPAGEI SAGT: SÜDEN IST DAS ZIEL
SCHON IMMER WOLLTEST DU DIE MEERE SEHEN

UND WENN DIE 7 WINDE WEHEN
BIST DU DER KÖNIG
DIE KÖNIGIN DER WELT
UND WENN DU EINMAL TRAURIG BIST
DER ALTE SEEBÄR
DER WEISS WAS DIR GEFÄLLT

DORT VORNE KANNST DU EINE INSEL SEHEN
HIER LEBT DER GROSSE RIESE POLYPHEM
ER WINKT DIR ZU MIT SEINER RIESENHAND
IHR SETZT DEN ANKER UND IHR GEHT AN LAND

DER RIESE FREUT SICH WIE EIN KLEINER THOR
ER STELLT EUCH SEINE INSELFREUNDE VOR
AM LAGERFEUER GRILLT ER MARSHMALLOWS
3 STUNDEN SPÄTER FAHRT IHR WIEDER LOS

UND WENN DIE 7 WINDE WEHEN
BIST DU DER KÖNIG
DIE KÖNIGIN DER WELT
UND WENN DU EINMAL TRAURIG BIST
DER ALTE SEEBÄR
DER WEISS WAS DIR GEFÄLLT

DON´T YOU DARE TO CINDERELLA JOHN

IN A GLORIOUS LAND
ON A STONY OLD ROAD
DAISY WAITING FOR JOHN
JOHN IS KISSING HIS DATE
DON´T YOU DARE TO CINDERELLA JOHN
IT´S TOO LATE

DRINKING WHISKY AND A GIN
JOHN AND DAISY MAKING LOVE
EVERYBODY IN THIS TOWN
KNOWS THE RULES AND GETS AWAY
DON´T YOU DARE TO CINDERELLA JOHN
FOR A DAY

READY TO GO, READY TO FLY
DAISY AND JOHN GIVE IT A TRY
DON´T YOU DARE TO CINDERELLA JOHN
FOR A RIDE

SUSIE LEAVING HER MAN
SHE´S A BEAUTY AND MORE
SEEING JOHN AND HIS DATE
SUSIE GETS UP ON STAGE
DON´T YOU DARE TO CINDERELLA JOHN
TURN THE PAGE

JOHN AND DAISY MAKING LOVE
SUSIE TAKING OFF HER TOP
JOHN IS GETTING IN A MESS
SUSIE GRABBING JOHNNYS COLT
DON´T YOU DARE TO CINDERELLA JOHN
SUSIE´S TOLD

READY TO GO, READY TO FLY
DAISY AND JOHN GIVE IT A TRY
DON´T YOU DARE TO CINDERELLA JOHN
SAY GOODBYE

FACE TO FACE – HAND IN HAND

FACE TO FACE – HAND IN HAND
WE SOLVED OUR PROBLEMS
THE WAY WE DO, THE WAY WE ARE, A PAIR OF GOLD
BACK TO BACK, TURNING ROUND, I WANNA KISS YOU
WE FIND A WAY ALTHOUGH WE LIVE
IN DIFFERENT WORLDS

2 ROOMS OF PEOPLE LIVING BY AND HAVE TO GET ALONG
SOMETIMES YOUR PRESENCE MAKES ME CRY
BUT I STAY STRONG

IN DIFFERENT TIMES OF FACE TO FACE
WHERE PEOPLE GET AWAY
A DARKER SIDE OF HUMAN RACE
WILL GET YOU DOWN
WE FIGHT THE DARKNESS HAND IN HAND
A SIGN OF LOVING YOU
WE STAY TOGETHER TIL THE END
WON´T LET YOU GO

NIGHT BY NIGHT, DAY TO DAY
WE SOLVE OUR PROBLEMS
I NEVER THOUGHT, I NEVER KNEW WE COULD BE STRONG
FACE TO FACE – HAND IN HAND UNTIL I´M LEAVING
WHERE I WILL GO, WHERE I WILL BE
I STILL DON´T KNOW

2 PEOPLE NEVER UNDERSTAND OF ALL THE HUMAN RACE
2 PEOPLE LIVING HAND IN HAND
BUT FACE TO FACE

IN DIFFERENT TIMES OF FACE TO FACE
WHERE PEOPLE GET AWAY
A DARKER SIDE OF HUMAN RACE
WILL GET YOU DOWN
WE FIGHT THE DARKNESS HAND IN HAND
A SIGN OF LOVING YOU
WE STAY TOGETHER TIL THE END
WON´T LET YOU GO

FIREFLY FUNHOUSE

WILL WE KISS AND WILL WE DO
THE THINGS I WANT TONIGHT?
WILL YOU BE WITH ME UNTIL
THE FIRST DAWN OF THE LIGHT?
WILL I BE A HAPPY MAN
FROM HEAD UP TO THE TOES?
WILL YOU BE MY SUPERGIRL?
YOU KNOW JUST HOW IT GOES

HOURS OF LOVETIME
CALLING TONIGHT
WILL YOU BE GRATEFUL
HERE AND TONIGHT?
HOURS OF MAGIC
NOT FAR AWAY
FIREFLY FUNHOUSE
LOVE ME TODAY

WILL WE BE A BROTHER AND A SISTER
OR A PAIR?
WILL YOU BE ATTRACTIVE
AS SOME LOVE IS IN THE AIR?
WILL YOU LOOK THE WAY YOU LOOK
INSIDE MY RUMBLING HEAD?
WILL WE TAKE THE CHANCE AND PLAY
SOME LOVE GAMES IN MY BED?

HOURS OF LOVETIME
CALLING TONIGHT
WILL YOU BE GRATEFUL
HERE AND TONIGHT?
HOURS OF MAGIC
NOT FAR AWAY
FIREFLY FUNHOUSE
LOVE ME TODAY

FLORENTINA

HEADACHE IN THE MORNING
DRINK A CUP OF COFFEE IN THE MORNING
YESTERDAY WAS SUCH A CRAZY DAY
KISSED MARIA IN THE MORNING
LEFT ANDREA IN THE DAWN AND
SPENT THE NIGHT WITH FLORENCE ANYWAY

NEVER BEEN A LONELY WALKER
NEVER BEEN A CRYING WALKER
I PREFER A LADY BY MY SIDE
NEVER BEEN A LOUSY LOVER
NEVER DATED LOUSY MOTHERS
LOOKING FOR A BABE WITH SUCH A RIDE

LOOKING FOR A CHALLENGE, MAYBE
WILL YOU BE MY CHALLENGE, BABY?
NEVER SEEN A GIRL LIKE YOU BEFORE
IF YOU´RE 18 CALL MY NUMBER
WE CAN HAVE ANOTHER NUMBER
ONE YOU WON´T FORGET AND STILL WANT MORE

ON MY WAY TO ANNA-LINA
ON MY WAY TO FLORENTINA
HORNY IS YOUR GIRLISH PRETTY FACE
NEVER BEEN A SLOWED DOWN LOVER
NEVER BEEN A LOW CLASS LOVER
I KNOW ALL THE TRICKS AND ALL THE WAYS

LADY, MAKE ME TURN AROUND
KISS ME DOWN ONTO THE GROUND
TAKE MY HEART AND MAKE ME
FLY WITH YOU INTO THE SKY

FREUNDSCHAFT, LIEBE UND GLÜCK

JA, DER REGENBOGEN IST SCHÖN
VON HIER UNTEN KANNST DU IHN SEHEN
WO ER ENDET IST NICHT BEKANNT
AUCH SEINEN START NOCH NIEMAND FAND

JA, DER REGENBOGEN IST SCHÖN
ALLE TIERE KÖNNEN IHN SEHEN
UND WER TRAURIG IST UND ALLEIN
DER KOMMT ZU MIR, ICH LASS IHN REIN

FREUNDSCHAFT, LIEBE UND GLÜCK
SCHENK ICH DIR
WAS DICH AUCH BEDRÜCKT
FREIHEIT UND HARMONIE
SPÜRST DU DIE KRAFT
DIE TIEF IN DIR SCHLIEF?
SEI BEREIT, DAS LEBEN IST SCHÖN
SO WUNDERSCHÖN!

JA, DAS LEBEN IST WUNDERSCHÖN
BESSER ALS IM REGEN ZU STEHEN
DRUM SEI STARK UND DENK POSITIV
DANN FINDEST DU DEIN PARADIES

BIST DU WÜTEND, WANDLE ES UM
IN DIE LIEBE, FRAG NICHT WARUM
SCHAU NACH VORN UND GIB EINFACH GAS
GREIF NACH DEM MOND, HAB GANZ VIEL SPASS

FREUNDSCHAFT, LIEBE UND GLÜCK
SCHENK ICH DIR
WAS DICH AUCH BEDRÜCKT
FREIHEIT UND HARMONIE
SPÜRST DU DIE KRAFT
DIE TIEF IN DIR SCHLIEF?
SEI BEREIT, DAS LEBEN IST SCHÖN
SO WUNDERSCHÖN!

G - L

GANGSTER IN THE HOUSE

IN THE DARK
A GANG IS ON THE STREET
A BRAIN, NO HEART
THEY´RE READY FOR A CHEAT
WALKING THROUGH A DOOR
I KNOW WAS CLOSED
THEY´RE FASTER THAN A GUN
AND MOVE LIKE GHOST

GANGSTER IN THE HOUSE, GANGSTER IN THE HOUSE
GANGSTER IN THE HOUSE, GANGSTER IN THE HOUSE
GANGSTER IN THE HOUSE, GANGSTER IN THE HOUSE
GANGSTER IN THE HOUSE, GANGSTER IN THE HOUSE

NEXT NIGHT NOW
THE SHADOWS BACK AGAIN
THEY DO IT NOW
THEY ROB A WEALTHY MAN
GANG IS ON THE STREET
SO I DO CARE
THE NEWSPAPER I READ
OF SUCH A SCARE

GANGSTER IN THE HOUSE, GANGSTER IN THE HOUSE
GANGSTER IN THE HOUSE, GANGSTER IN THE HOUSE
GANGSTER IN THE HOUSE, GANGSTER IN THE HOUSE
GANGSTER IN THE HOUSE, GANGSTER IN THE HOUSE

KNIFES AND FORKS
I KNOW WHAT THEY PRETEND
NO CATS, NO DOGS
CAN HELP THE OWNER MAN
STRONGER THAN A BRICK
AND RICH LIKE GOLD
THE CITY OF THE SICK
I NEED TO GO

GANGSTER IN THE HOUSE, GANGSTER IN THE HOUSE
GANGSTER IN THE HOUSE, GANGSTER IN THE HOUSE
GANGSTER IN THE HOUSE, GANGSTER IN THE HOUSE
GANGSTER IN THE HOUSE, GANGSTER IN THE HOUSE

GEBURTSTAGSKIND

EINMAL NUR IM JAHR HAST DU GEBURTSTAG
AN DIESEM TAG WIRST DU BESCHENKT
DU BIST DER STAR
UND ALLE KINDER WÜNSCHEN DIR EIN SCHÖNES LEBEN
SIE SCHENKEN DIR GANZ TOLLE SACHEN
DIE DU MAGST

BALD SCHON KOMMT DER TAG AN DEM DU FEIERST
DIE SPANNUNG STEIGT
UND DU BIST REICHER UM 1 JAHR
SOGAR DIE OMAS SIND GEKOMMEN MIT DEN OPAS
UND ALLE FEIERN JETZT MIT DIR
DEN GANZEN TAG

GEBURTSTAGSKIND, DAS BESTE WÜNSCH ICH DIR
HAB EINEN WUNDERSCHÖNEN TAG UND SING MIT MIR
WELL, HAPPY BIRTHDAY, MY DEAR
SPRING UND TANZ MIT MIR
GEBURTSTAG IST EINMAL IM JAHR

LECKER DUFTET SCHON DER MARMORKUCHEN
JETZT HOL TIEF LUFT
UND BLAS DIE GANZEN KERZEN AUS
AUCH DEINE TANTEN UND DIE ONKEL SIND GEBLIEBEN
SIE SITZEN AUF DEM SOFA
UND RUHEN SICH JETZT AUS

EINMAL NUR IM JAHR HAST DU GEBURTSTAG
ES IST SOWEIT, DIE PARTY STEIGT
JETZT GEHT ES LOS!
UND ALLE KINDER WÜNSCHEN DIR EIN LANGES LEBEN
HEUT IST DEIN EHRENTAG
DRUM TU NUR WAS DU MAGST

GEBURTSTAGSKIND, DAS BESTE WÜNSCH ICH DIR
HAB EINEN WUNDERSCHÖNEN TAG UND SING MIT MIR
WELL, HAPPY BIRTHDAY, MY DEAR
SPRING UND TANZ MIT MIR
GEBURTSTAG IST EINMAL IM JAHR

GÖTTINNEN

DIE JAHRE VERGEHEN
UND ICH WEISS ES IMMER NOCH NICHT
MACH ICH´S ALLEN RECHT
UND SCHAU ICH WIRKLICH ZU WENIG AUF MICH?
WER BIN ICH? WAS BIN ICH? WARUM BIN ICH?

KENN ICH MEINEN KÖRPER
ODER IST ES EINFACH SO?
KENN ICH MEINE WÜNSCHE
ODER BIN ICH AUCH SO FROH?
LASS ICH MANCHMAL LOS
UND DENK AB JETZT DARAN
ICH BIN EINE GÖTTIN UND KEIN MANN

GÖTTINNEN SIND LEBHAFT, GÖTTINNEN SIND HELL
GÖTTINNEN SIND AUFGESCHLOSSEN
UND SEHR VISUELL
GÖTTINNEN SIND INTERESSIERT
UND MACHEN WAS SIE WOLLEN
WIR SIND EINZIGARTIG, GÖTTINNEN SIND TOLL

KENN ICH DIE HORMONE
UND WEISS ICH WAS SIE SO TUN?
KENN ICH MEINE WERTE
ODER STREB ICH NUR NACH RUHM?
LASS ICH MANCHMAL LOS
UND DENK EINFACH DARAN
ICH BIN EINE GÖTTIN UND KEIN MANN

GÖTTINNEN SIND LIEBENSWERT, GÖTTINNEN SIND FEIN
GÖTTINNEN SIND AUFGESCHLOSSEN
UND NICHT GERN ALLEIN
GÖTTINNEN SIND INTERESSIERT
UND MACHEN WAS SIE WOLLEN
WIR SIND EINZIGARTIG, GÖTTINNEN SIND TOLL

SCHWITZEN, FRIEREN, STIMMUNGSSCHWANKEN
ESSEN, TRINKEN, FRUSTGEDANKEN
HIMMELHOCH JAUCHZEND UND ZU TODE BETRÜBT
ICH BIN EINE GÖTTIN UND ICH WERD VON DIR GELIEBT

GYPSY GIRLS & BONGO BOYS

GYPSY GIRLS AND BONGO BOYS ARE DANCING
WINDS OF JOY ARE FLYING THROUGH THE AIR
ON THIS ISLE OF LOVE AND SWEET ROMANCING
PRETTY FACES SMILING EVERYWHERE

SUDDENLY A BIG MYSTERIOUS WOMAN
SCREAMING WORDS OF WISDOM IN MY FACE
SHE IS WAITING FOR HER CRAZY CREWMEN
DRINKING BLOOD AND SMOKING YELLOW HAZE

THE GYPSY GIRLS WON´T GO AWAY
SHE IS THEIR LEADER SO TO SAY
AND ALL THE HELPLESS BONGO BOYS
I KNOW THEY HAVE NO OTHER CHOICE

GYPSY GIRLS AND BONGO BOYS ARE SCREAMING
CAN YOU HEAR THEIR MESSAGE IN THE NIGHT?
MOST OF THEM ARE DREAMING DREAMS OF LEAVING
PRISONED IN A WORLD OF LOVE AND LIGHT

AS THIS REALLY MIGHTY GYPSY WOMAN
DRINKING BLOOD AND SMOKING YELLOW HAZE
I NOW TAKE THE CHANCE TO SAY GOODBYE THEN
LEAVING NOW THIS SPOOKY GYPSY PLACE

THE GYPSY GIRLS WON´T GO AWAY
SHE IS THEIR LEADER SO TO SAY
AND ALL THE HELPLESS BONGO BOYS
I KNOW THEY HAVE NO OTHER CHOICE

I ASK YOU THIS

CAN YOU JUMP A HUNDRED METER FROM THE START?
CAN YOU MAKE A BABY JUST WITH 2?
I ASK YOU THIS

CAN YOU RUN SOME HUNDRED THOUSAND MILES A DAY?
CAN YOU FLY WITHOUT A BOING PLANE?
I ASK YOU THIS

NO, YOU CAN´T
SO I DON´T FOLLOW ALL YOUR STUPID LIES
NEVER HEARD OF SUCH PSYCHOLOGY
BETTER CLOSE THE DOOR
AND DO THE THINGS YOU LIKE IN FANTASY
NEVER EVER REALLY IN SOME HUNDRED TAKES OF LIVES
WILL YOU BE THE ONE YOU THINK YOU ARE
CRAZY IN YOUR MIND
BUT STILL YOU CARRY ON YOUR SELFMADE STAR

CAN YOU BUILD A HOUSE IN JUST ANOTHER DAY?
CAN YOU KISS A LION ON HIS MOUTH?
I ASK YOU THIS

CAN YOU LIVE FOREVER LIKE A WATERFALL?
CAN YOU SMOKE A SNAKE AROUND YOUR HEAD?
I ASK YOU THIS

NO, YOU CAN´T
SO I DON´T FOLLOW ALL YOUR STUPID LIES
NEVER HEARD OF SUCH PSYCHOLOGY
BETTER CLOSE THE DOOR
AND DO THE THINGS YOU LIKE IN FANTASY
NEVER EVER REALLY IN SOME HUNDRED TAKES OF LIVES
WILL YOU BE THE ONE YOU THINK YOU ARE
CRAZY IN YOUR MIND
BUT STILL YOU CARRY ON YOUR SELFMADE STAR

YOU´RE KILLING MY TIME
YOU´RE DRIFTING AWAY
YOU´RE LOSING YOUR LIFE
AND IT´S TOO LATE

I SAID RED AND YOU SAID BLACK

I WILL GO
EARLY MORNING
I WILL LEAVE, GO AWAY
THOUGH I´M SAD
I WON´T MISS YOU
ALL THE WORDS YOU DON´T SAY

IT´S OKAY
NOW YOU HATE ME
IT´S OKAY, I DON´T MIND
WON´T COME BACK
NEVER EVER
SOMEONE NEW I WILL FIND

I SAID RED AND YOU SAID BLACK
I WAS SLEEPING WHEN YOU WENT AWAY
I WENT FORTH AND YOU WENT BACK
NO SECRET WITH ANOTHER MAN
THE LOVE WILL NEVER COME AGAIN

IT´S SO STRANGE
I FEEL LUCKY
IT´S SO STRANGE HOW I FEEL
NO MORE LOVE
BUT I´M HAPPY
IN MY MIND STILL UNREAL

I SAID RED AND YOU SAID BLACK
I WAS SLEEPING WHEN YOU WENT AWAY
I WENT FORTH AND YOU WENT BACK
NO SECRET WITH ANOTHER MAN
THE LOVE WILL NEVER COME AGAIN

I´M PAINTING YOUR CANDY

PAINT THE COLOUR OF YOU
IS IT BLUE, STRAWBERRY OR WHITE?
PAINT A PICTURE OF YOU
HERE AND TONIGHT

NOW TAKE OFF ALL YOUR CLOTHES
AND I TRY MY BEST TO BE TRUE
WITH THE COLOUR I LIKE
I´M PAINTING YOU

IT´S A MIRACLE
IT´S SO MYSTHICAL
IT´S THE MAGIC OF LIFE
IT´S SO BEAUTIFUL
IT´S SO MAGICAL
IT´S SO STRONG AND ALIVE
THE BEAUTY I SEE IN YOUR EYES
I´M PAINTING YOUR CANDY TONIGHT

PAINT THE COLOUR OF YOU
IS IT BLACK, BANANA OR BLUE?
PAINT A PICTURE OF LOVE
OF ME AND YOU

NOW TURN OFF ALL THE LIGHT
DEEP INSIDE A HUG AND A KISS
GUESS THAT´S ALL WHAT YOU LIKE
SWEET TENDERNESS

YOU´RE A MIRACLE
YOU´RE SO MYSTHICAL
YOU´RE THE MAGIC OF LIFE
YOU´RE SO BEAUTIFUL
YOU´RE SO MAGICAL
YOU´RE SO HOT AND ALIVE
THE BEAUTY I SEE IN YOUR EYES
I´M PAINTING YOUR CANDY TONIGHT

ISLAND OF LOVE

OPEN YOUR EYES IN PARADISE
MY CHRISTINE
PUT ON YOUR RED SOLERO
AND COME TO ME
ISLAND OF LOVE
SOME GAMES IN THE WHITEFUL SAND
READY TO SEE THE STARS
IN THIS RIGHTFUL LAND

COCONUT TREES
AND APPLE PIE IN THE GREEN
OPEN YOUR EYES IN PARADISE
SWEET CHRISTINE
MONKEYS ON TREES
AND DINOSAURS ALL AROUND
OPEN YOUR EYES
THIS PARADISE I HAVE FOUND

HONEY AND I ENJOYING THIS WHISKY NIGHT
LEAVING BEHIND THE TEARS AND THE FEARS OF LIFE
NEVER AGAIN WILL I DIE OF TRAGEDY
MAKING A START IN THIS LAND OF FANTASY

OPEN YOUR EYES IN PARADISE
MY CHRISTINE
NEVER IN YEARS
THIS PICTURE WAS TO BE SEEN
PINEAPPLE DRINKS
AND CHUPA CHUPS EVERY DAY
HARMONY, LOVE AND FREEDOM
JUST ALL THE WAY

HONEY AND I ENJOYING THIS WHISKY NIGHT
LEAVING BEHIND THE TEARS AND THE FEARS OF LIFE
NEVER AGAIN WILL I DIE OF TRAGEDY
MAKING A START IN THIS LAND OF FANTASY

IT´S ALIVE!

TELL ME IT´S ALIVE
READY AND ALIVE
NO ONE WILL BE SAFE
WHEN IT COMES

SHOW ME IT´S ALIVE
HUNGRY AND ALIVE
MANKIND WILL BE FORCED
USING GUNS

ONE THING THEY DON´T KNOW
IS THEY WILL DIE
IF THEY TRY TO KILL IT
THEY WILL FLY
I´VE SEEN THIS BEAST EYE TO EYE
EARTHQUAKE AND LOVE IF THEY TRY

TRUST ME IT´S ALIVE
HAUNTING, SO ALIVE
BETTER RUN AWAY
WHEN IT COMES

SHOWDOWN IN THE NIGHT
SHOTGUNS IN THE NIGHT
DANGER FOR THE BRAVE
AND THEIR SONS

ONE THING THEY DON´T KNOW
IS THEY WILL DIE
IF THEY TRY TO KILL IT
THEY WILL FLY
I´VE SEEN THIS BEAST EYE TO EYE
EARTHQUAKE AND LOVE IF THEY TRY

LADY MACBETH

DOWN AT THE OPERA
WHERE THE PLAYERS HIDE IN THE DARK
THERE IS A MURDERER
OUT OF STORY BROKE ANOTHER HEART

I SAW AN EMPTY FACE
I PREPARED TO GET UP ON STAGE
I SAW HIM LYING THERE
IN A POOL OF BLOOD AND HELPLESS RAGE

LADY MACBETH
NOW WHERE ARE YOU NOW?
THE CREW IS SAVE, HE´S DOWN AND OUT
LADY MACBETH
IS THE ONLY ONE
WHO´S MISSING NOW, SHE´S REALLY GONE

NO ONE WAS NEAR ENOUGH
JUST TO SEE WHAT HAPPENED TO HIM
NOW IT IS CLEAR ENOUGH
MR. HENDRIX NEVER COMING IN

DOWN AT THE OPERA
ALL THE PLAYERS HIDE IN THE DARK
CAUSE THERE´S A MURDERER
AS WE SEE JIM HENDRIXS BROKEN HEART

LADY MACBETH
NOW WHERE ARE YOU NOW?
THE CREW IS SAVE, HE´S DOWN AND OUT
LADY MACBETH
IS THE ONLY ONE
WHO´S MISSING NOW, SHE´S REALLY GONE

LADYBOYS AND GEISHAS

NEVER BEEN TO TOKYO
NEXT YEAR I WANNA TRY
FLY ACROSS THE OCEAN IN THE SKY
LOOKING FOR A GEISHA
WANNA TRY A LADYBOY
DIDN´T TRIED BEFORE, I WAS TOO SHY

NEVER BEEN IN TOKYO
I´M FLYING TO JAPAN
WANT A BIG ADVENTURE CAUSE I CAN
SUSHI I DON´T EAT
AND I DON´T NEED TO SEE THIS LAND
LADYBOYS AND GEISHAS, HERE I AM

RIGHT INSIDE A LADYBOY
I CUM IN TOKYO
IT´S SO SPECIAL, I ENJOY THE SHOW
AND A PRETTY GEISHA
MAKING ME A MODERN MAN
BIG ADVENTURES WAITING IN THIS LAND

NEVER KISSED IN TOKYO BEFORE
SO HERE I AM
FLY ACROSS THE OCEAN TO JAPAN
WANNA MEET AND GREET
AND WANNA MAKE LOVE EVERY NIGHT
ARE YOU A CONTENDER FOR TONIGHT?

RIGHT INSIDE A LADYBOY
I CUM IN TOKYO
IT´S SO SPECIAL, I ENJOY THE SHOW
AND A PRETTY GEISHA
MAKING ME A MODERN MAN
BIG ADVENTURES WAITING IN THIS LAND

ON MY WAY TO SUPERMAN
I FIND OUT WHAT I CAN
IF YOU TRY TO FOLLOW ME
YOU´RE IN BED NOW WITH ME

LEBE DEINE TRÄUME

LEBE DEINE TRÄUME
WIE AUCH PETER PAN ES TAT
KOMM MIT AUF EINE REISE
IN DAS SCHÖNE NIMMERLAND

FEUERROTE HAARE
SPITZE OHREN SO WIE DU
DIE LUST AUF ABENTEUER
STECKT SIE AUCH GANZ TIEF IN DIR?

WIE EIN KIND SCHON MORGEN
ZUM KÖNIG WIRD
UND ICH BEGLEITE DICH
DENN DIE KRAFT IN DIR
KANN DIE WELT BEWEGEN
KOMM UND VERSTECK DICH NICHT

LEBE DEINE TRÄUME
PIPPILOTTA MACHT ES VOR
DAS STÄRKSTE MÄDCHEN IST SIE
HAT NOCH NIE EIN SPIEL VERLOREN

MUT IST IHRE TUGEND
IN DER VILLA KUNTERBUNT
DORT TREIBT SIE IHRE SPÄSSE
DENN VIEL LACHEN IST GESUND

WIE EIN KIND SCHON MORGEN
ZUM KÖNIG WIRD
UND ICH BEGLEITE DICH
DENN DIE KRAFT IN DIR
KANN DIE WELT BEWEGEN
KOMM UND VERSTECK DICH NICHT

LOOKING FOR A PARADISE

REMEMBER ALL THE DAYS YOU HAD BEFORE
AND NOW THE DAYS AHEAD
REMEMBER ALL THE MEN WHO TOOK THE DOOR
THEY LEFT YOU IN YOUR BED

ALL THE SCENES OF SADNESS
ALL THE SCENES OF MADNESS, THEY WILL FLY AWAY
ALL THE TEARS OF SORROW
KILLING THE TOMORROW, PRISONED IN A DAY

LOOKING FOR A PARADISE
I UNDERSTAND, I UNDERSTAND
SPARKLING MAGIC IN YOUR EYES
I AM YOUR FRIEND, I AM YOUR FRIEND
AS THE WORLD IS CHANGING NOW
TO SOMETHING GOOD, TO SOMETHING GOOD
LET ME TAKE YOU BY THE HAND
JUST LIKE I SHOULD, JUST LIKE I SHOULD

REMEMBER ALL THE NIGHTS YOU HAD BEFORE
THEY WERE NOT GOOD ENOUGH
REMEMBER ALL THE MEN BEHAVING BORED
AND YOU JUST BEING TOUGH

ALL THE SCENES OF TRAGIC
WISHING THEY WERE MAGIC NEVER SEEN BEFORE
ALL THE SCENES OF GIVING
NEVER EVER LIVING, LEAVING THROUGH THE DOOR

LOOKING FOR A PARADISE
I UNDERSTAND, I UNDERSTAND
SPARKLING MAGIC IN YOUR EYES
I AM YOUR FRIEND, I AM YOUR FRIEND
AS THE WORLD IS CHANGING NOW
TO SOMETHING GOOD, TO SOMETHING GOOD
LET ME TAKE YOU BY THE HAND
JUST LIKE I SHOULD, JUST LIKE I SHOULD

LOTTA, DIE LOGORAFFE

LOTTA, DIE LOGORAFFE
KLINGELT AN DER TÜR
LOTTA, DIE LOGORAFFE
BRINGT GESCHENKE DIR
LOTTA, DIE LOGORAFFE
FREUT SICH DICH ZU SEHEN
DU ZEIGST IHR GLEICH DEIN ZIMMER
UND SIE MACHT SICH'S BEQUEM

LOTTA, DIE LOGORAFFE
KANN AUF BÄUME SEHEN
LOTTA, DIE LOGORAFFE
KANN DEN HALS UMDREHEN
LOTTA, DIE LOGORAFFE
SCHIESST MIT LINKS EIN TOR
JA, SPORTLICH IST DIE LOTTA
SIE TURNT DIR WAS VOR

LOTTA, DIE LOGORAFFE KENNT DEN POLYPHEM
LOTTA, DIE LOGORAFFE KANN DIE STERNE ZÄHLEN
LOTTA, DIE LOGORAFFE
IST DA WENN DU SIE BRAUCHST
UND MIR UND DEM RIESEN HILFT SIE AUCH

LOTTA, DIE LOGORAFFE
HALF AUCH CHARLY SPATZ
DER LIEBT NUN SEINE STÖRCHIN
UND IM NEST IST PLATZ
CHARLY, DU MÖCHTEST KINDER
7 AN DER ZAHL
DIE LOTTA WIRD DANN OMA
UND DU DER PAPA

LOTTA, DIE LOGORAFFE KANN AUF BÄUME SEHEN
LOTTA, DIE LOGORAFFE KANN DEN HALS UMDREHEN
LOTTA, DIE LOGORAFFE
SCHIESST AUCH MIT RECHTS EIN TOR
DU SINGST LAUT UND TANZT IHR JETZT WAS VOR

LOVE I HAVE FOUND

OPEN UP YOUR EYES AND HOLD ME CLOSE
YESTERDAY WE HAD TOO MUCH OF WINE
QUITE SOMEHOW WE ENDED IN THIS BED
HAD A NIGHT OF JOY ´FORE SLEEPING TIME

DON´T ASK ME NOW
IF WE CROSSED THE DREADED LINE
DON´T ASK ME NOW
CAUSE WE´RE HAVING A GOOD TIME
A BEST-OF-FRIEND THING IT WAS UNTIL THIS NIGHT

TURN AROUND, LOVE I HAVE FOUND
IT IS SO EASY NOW
TO EXPRESS MY WORLD OF LOVE
YESTERDAY FINDING OUR WAY
I NEVER THOUGHT WE COULD BE
TOGETHER LIKE THE STARS

OPEN UP YOUR EYES AND HOLD ME TIGHT
CHANGING NOW THE CHAPTER OF OUR BOOK
THOUGH I´VE SEEN YOU NAKED ALL BEFORE
NEVER KNEW YOU TASTED OH SO GOOD

LET´S CALL IT LOVE
AT THE SECOND SIGHT OF LIFE
WELL, IT´S YOUR LOVE
FLOWING THROUGH MY VEINS OF LIFE
WE´RE GONNA LIVE NOW TOGETHER AS THEY SAY

TURN AROUND, LOVE I HAVE FOUND
IT IS SO EASY NOW
TO EXPRESS MY WORLD OF LOVE
YESTERDAY FINDING OUR WAY
I NEVER THOUGHT WE COULD BE
TOGETHER LIKE THE STARS

LUCKILY I´M ON MY WAY

LOVE ISN´T IN MY LIFE
ISN´T IN MY HEART
THOUGH I´M HARDLY TRYING
TIME ISN´T ON MY SIDE
ISN´T PLAYING OUT
STICKY TEARS I´M CRYING

TRIED WHAT I COULDN´T TRY
WHAT I COULDN´T DO
LIKE THERE´S NO TOMORROW
FOUGHT WHAT I COULDN´T FIGHT
DIDN´T WANT TO HIDE
ALL MY TEARS OF SORROW

LUCKILY I´M ON MY WAY
PRAYING FOR A BETTER DAY
I NEVER HAD THE CHANCES
OF A PLAYBOY OR A MILLIONAIRE
LEAVING NOW THE PAST BEHIND
PRAYING FOR A STRONGER MIND
I´M HAPPY ON MY WAY
I KNOW THE PROBLEMS ARE NO LONGER THERE

LOVE WASN´T IN MY LIFE
WASN´T IN MY HEART
BUT MY FUTURE´S SHINING
FUN, I WILL HAVE SOME FUN
I WILL BE THE ONE
THAT IS ALWAYS SMILING

LUCKILY I´M ON MY WAY
PRAYING FOR A BETTER DAY
I NEVER HAD THE CHANCES
OF A PLAYBOY OR A MILLIONAIRE
LEAVING NOW THE PAST BEHIND
PRAYING FOR A STRONGER MIND
I´M HAPPY ON MY WAY
I KNOW THE PROBLEMS ARE NO LONGER THERE

M - Q

MAGIC UNDERNEATH MY BED

UNDERNEATH THIS LITTLE BED OF MINE
THERE IS A CORNY DOOR
INTO THE GREEN
EVERY NIGHT I CANNOT SLEEP INSIDE
THE DOOR GETS OPEN WIDE
AND I MUST GO

AS I GO INTO THIS LAND OF MINE
INTO ANOTHER TIME
A DIFFERENT PLACE
I JUST FEEL I´M GETTING CLOSER TO
THE LAND OF FANTASY
I´M HERE AGAIN

MAGIC UNDERNEATH MY BED
IS NEVER COMING BACK
THEREFORE I WILL MAKE THIS JOURNEY
NOT JUST IN MY HEAD
WHEN THE DOOR WILL FADE AWAY
I WILL BE THERE ENJOYING NOW MY DAY

WHEN I WAS A BOY OF 3 OR 4
I FOUND THE MAGIC DOOR
TO PARADISE
EVERY NIGHT I COULDN´T SLEEP INSIDE
THE DOOR GOT OPEN WIDE
FOR ME TO GO

MAGIC UNDERNEATH MY BED
IS NEVER COMING BACK
THEREFORE I WILL MAKE THIS JOURNEY
NOT JUST IN MY HEAD
WHEN THE DOOR WILL FADE AWAY
I WILL BE THERE ENJOYING NOW MY DAY

MAKING LOVE ON SATURDAY

I KNOW THAT OUR LOVE IS OVER
I KNOW THAT OUR LOVE HAS GONE
SO MAYBE IT´S JUST THE WEEKENDS
WE COULD USE FOR A NIGHT OF FUN
DON´T DISRESPECT ME FOR THINKING
IN BED WE FIT PERFECTLY
AND THOUGH OUR LOVE NOW IS OVER
WE SHOULD TRY IT, DON´T YOU AGREE?

LOOKING FOR THE SATURDAY
THE DOOR IS RINGING, JUST COME IN
WAITING FOR A HAPPENING
GET READY, I´M COMING IN
MAKING LOVE ON SATURDAY
THE MAGIC IS STILL WITH US
DON´T YOU CARE YOU LIVE ALONG
WITH BENNY LAMAR, YOUR BOSS

MY BODY IS GETTING OLDER
YOUR BODY IS STILL IN SHAPE
AND STILL IT IS ALL THE WEEKENDS
WHEN WE GIVE AWAY AND WE TAKE
ALTHOUGH YOU ARE PROUDLY MARRIED
ALTHOUGH YOU HAVE CHILDREN TOO
OUR MAGIC IS EVEN STRONGER
AND I WANNA HAVE FUN WITH YOU

LOOKING FOR THE SATURDAY
THE DOOR IS RINGING, JUST COME IN
WAITING FOR A HAPPENING
GET READY, I´M COMING IN
MAKING LOVE ON SATURDAY
THE MAGIC IS STILL WITH US
DON´T YOU CARE YOU LIVE ALONG
WITH BENNY LAMAR, YOUR BOSS

MAN OF ROCK AND ROLL

A MAN OF ROCK AND ROLL I AM
THE MUSIC I BELIEVE
IS HARDER THAN BALLADS IN THE NIGHT
MY TELECASTER FENDER
IS A ONE OF ´65
MY JEANS ARE ALL DIRTY IN THE LIGHT

A MAN OF ROCK AND ROLL
IS SO MUCH BIGGER AS YOU ARE
MY SILVER HAIR SHINING IN THE LIGHT
SOME SMOKE IS ON THE WATER
AND I SOMETIMES BREAK THE RULES
I´M ROCKING AWAY INTO THE NIGHT

A GOD OF ROCK AND ROLL, A SUPERMAN
WHEN I AWAKE I´M ROCKING ON
SOME GIRLS OF 18 LOVE A ROCKING MAN
IT´S SO MUCH FUN

A MAN OF ROCK AND ROLL
IS PLAYING RIFFS INTO YOUR EARS
YOU´RE DANCING SO SEXY TO THE BEAT
I´M QUITE INTERESTED IN THIS LADY
STARING UP AT ME
I´M ROCKING ON TO FULFILL MY NEED

THE MAN OF ROCK AND ROLL
IS GETTING OLDER DAY BY DAY
HIS FENDER IS NEARLY BROKEN DOWN
2000 GIRLS AND LADIES
GOT THE MAN OF ROCK AND ROLL
AND STILL THERE ARE HUNGRY CHICKS AROUND

A GOD OF ROCK AND ROLL, A SUPERMAN
WHEN I AWAKE I´M ROCKING ON
SOME GIRLS OF 18 LOVE A ROCKING MAN
IT´S SO MUCH FUN

MAYBE THE TIME AND YOU HAVE CHANGED

I NEVER SAW
THE ANGER IN YOUR EYES
I NEVER THOUGHT
YOU COULD BE OH SO CRUEL
THE YEARS WE LIVED
TOGETHER SIDE BY SIDE
I NEVER SAW YOU PLAYING THE FOOL

MAYBE THE TIME AND YOU HAVE CHANGED
I NEED TO KNOW WHAT´S GOING ON
MAYBE A LITTLE BIT DERANGED
I NEVER SAW SUCH CREEPY FUN

BRUTALITY
WAS NEVER IN YOUR FACE
I NEVER THOUGHT OF YOU
A KILLER QUEEN
IT MUST HAVE BEEN
A DREADED TIME AND PLACE
RESPONSIBLE FOR WHAT I HAVE SEEN

MAYBE THE TIME AND YOU HAVE CHANGED
I NEED TO KNOW WHAT´S GOING ON
MAYBE A LITTLE BIT DERANGED
I NEVER SAW SUCH CREEPY FUN

WHAT IS NOW THE TRUTH?
I NEED AN ANSWER
IS IT WIN OR LOSE
FOR YOU AGAIN?

MICHELANGELO SAID

IN A WORLD OF FIGHTING DYING
PEOPLE ALL AROUND ARE LYING
NO ONE WANTS TO LEAVE THIS PLANET
TIME IS UP, THEY FALL IN PANIC

LIVING IN A WORLD OF EGO
HELPING IS A BIG BLACK NO GO
SMOKING CIGARETTES AND DRINKING
ALCOHOL WITHOUT JUST THINKING

SO I DECIDED TO RISE UP INSTEAD
I FOLLOW WORDS
MICHELANGELO SAID
MY LIFE IS MORE THAN A SIMPLE NIGHT STAND
I KNOW SOME TIME
I AM LEAVING THIS LAND

MAYBE IT´S A THING OF 5G
MAKING ALL THE PEOPLE CRAZY
MAYBE IT´S THE DREADED TV
SHOWING PEOPLE HOW THEY SHOULD BE

IN A WORLD OF FIGHTING DYING
PEOPLE ALL AROUND ARE LYING
NO ONE WANTS TO LEAVE THIS PLANET
TIME IS UP, THEY FALL IN PANIC

SO I DECIDED TO RISE UP INSTEAD
I FOLLOW WORDS
MICHELANGELO SAID
MY LIFE IS MORE THAN A SIMPLE NIGHT STAND
I KNOW SOME TIME
I AM LEAVING THIS LAND

NIGHTMARE AIN´T A SECOND CHANCE

ANOTHER DAY, ANOTHER NIGHT
ANOTHER SWEET REVENGE
ANOTHER GIRL, ANOTHER FACE
ANOTHER CIRCUMSTANCE
ANOTHER PLACE, ANOTHER TIME, ANOTHER HOTEL ROOM
ANOTHER BED, ANOTHER LADY NOW THIS AFTERNOON

ANOTHER KISS, ANOTHER TALK
ANOTHER RENDEZVOUS
ANOTHER GLASS OF WINE
ANOTHER DINNER DATE FOR 2
ANOTHER CASANOVA TRICK, ANOTHER VIDEO
ANOTHER PRIVATE MOVIE, I ENJOY TO WATCH THE SHOW

NIGHTMARE AIN´T A SECOND CHANCE
I DO LOOK BACK ON MY WAY
ALL THE PRETTY GIRLS I HAD
I TAKE ´EM BACK FOR A DAY

ANOTHER HIGHLIGHT
AND ANOTHER HIGHLIGHT ON MY WAY
ANOTHER ROOM, ANOTHER SCREAM
ANOTHER BIG HURRAY
ANOTHER NIGHT TOGETHER AND ANOTHER NIGHT OF JOY
ANOTHER EARLY MORNING I WAKE UP A HAPPY BOY

ANOTHER SEXY BODY
AND ANOTHER TONGUEY TOUCH
ANOTHER RIDE, ANOTHER RIDE
ANOTHER LOVELY CLUTCH
ANOTHER BIG EXPERIENCE I HAVE ON VIDEO
ANOTHER PRIVATE MOVIE, I ENJOY TO WATCH THE SHOW

NIGHTMARE AIN´T A SECOND CHANCE
I DO LOOK BACK ON MY WAY
ALL THE PRETTY GIRLS I HAD
I TAKE ´EM BACK FOR A DAY

NIGHTSCARE

TURN AROUND, TURN AWAY
BETTER NOW HEAR THE CALL
RUN AWAY, RUN AROUND
OTHERWISE YOU WILL FALL

SHAKING
THE WORLD IS BREAKING AWAY
MAKING A SCENE OF FLYING AWAY
I REALLY GO AS THE FIRST ONE OF THIS TOWN
NIGHTMARE
THE DARKNESS HOLDING YOU CLOSE
NIGHTSCARE
I FEEL I´M LEAVING ALONE
THE PANIC FLIES
LIKE A DEMON IN THE NIGHT

FOLLOW ME, FOLLOW ME
LEAVING THIS PLACE FOR SURE
HISTORY CHANGING ME
ALL OF THIS LAND AND MORE

SHAKING
THE WORLD IS BREAKING AWAY
MAKING A SCENE OF FLYING AWAY
I REALLY GO AS THE FIRST ONE OF THIS TOWN
NIGHTMARE
THE DARKNESS HOLDING YOU CLOSE
NIGHTSCARE
I FEEL I´M LEAVING ALONE
THE PANIC FLIES
LIKE A DEMON IN THE NIGHT

ON THE HILL OF LOVE

THE TIME WAS GOOD
THE TIME WAS BAD NOT FOR ME
WE KISSED AND TALKED
THE DAY AWAY AT THE SEA

BUT WHEN THE SUN CHANGED TO YELLOW
FOR GOODBYE
I TOOK YOU WITH ME TO SHOW YOU
THE SPARKLING SKY

ON THE HILL OF LOVE
NO WORDS IN MY EAR, JUST SHOOTING STARS
I DON´T KNOW YOUR NAME
BUT I JUST KNOW HOW YOU FEEL
WELL, THIS NIGHT WILL BE SO SPECIAL
JUST LIKE A WANDERER
COMING HOME, A TRIP OF SADNESS
HE´D LEFT BEHIND

I HAD MY TIME
BUT ENDED UP IN THE RAIN
I´D LOST MY JOB
MY GIRL, MY LIFE AND MY FAME

AND THEN I LEFT FOR A JOURNEY
TO THE SEA
AND NOW I´M WITH YOU
PLEASE TELL ME YOU LIKE TO BE

ON THE HILL OF LOVE
NO WORDS IN MY EAR, JUST SHOOTING STARS
I DON´T KNOW YOUR NAME
BUT I JUST KNOW HOW YOU FEEL
WELL, THIS NIGHT WILL BE SO SPECIAL
JUST LIKE A WANDERER
COMING HOME, A TRIP OF SADNESS
HE´D LEFT BEHIND

ONCE I WAS SO IN LOVE WITH YOU

CAN´T SEE YOUR FACE
EVERY NIGHT ANYMORE
WATCHING TV ALL THE TIME
YOU IGNORE
WE´RE STILL A PAIR
BUT YOU LIVE JUST YOUR LIFE
FEEDING YOURSELF
WITH YOUR SWEETS ALL THE TIME

ONCE I WAS SO IN LOVE WITH YOU
PALE IS NOW YOUR FACE
ONCE I WAS SO ATTACHED TO YOU
GOLDEN LOVELY DAYS
LOOK AT YOU, YOU´RE A BOOGER NOW
DULL AND OUT OF SHAPE
THEREFORE NOW I WILL WALK AWAY
ENDING OUR DAYS

LIKE YOU HAVE CHANGED
I HAVE NOT SEEN BEFORE
YOU KICKED OUR LIFE
I DON´T LOVE YOU NO MORE
LOST IN YOUR MIND
I PREFER NOW TO GO
DON´T WANNA SEE
YOU AGAIN ANYMORE

ONCE I WAS SO IN LOVE WITH YOU
PALE IS NOW YOUR FACE
ONCE I WAS SO ATTACHED TO YOU
GOLDEN LOVELY DAYS
LOOK AT YOU, YOU´RE A BOOGER NOW
DULL AND OUT OF SHAPE
THEREFORE NOW I WILL WALK AWAY
ENDING OUR DAYS

ORLANDO WASN´T DEAD BEFORE

I´M A LITTLE LOVER AS THE WORLD IS GOING BY
HAILSTONES AND A LOT UP IN THE SKY
THUNDER AND THE RAIN
ARE STRONG ENOUGH TO CALL THE BELL
TAKING PRETTY FLOWERS INTO HELL

I´M A LITTLE LOVER AS THE WORLD IS GOING BY
MAYBE THERE´S A CHANCE FOR ME TO FLY
I´M LOOKING OUT THE WINDOW
AND THE WORLD IS IN A MESS
I KEEP ON GOING STRONG, I GIVE MY BEST

ORLANDO WASN´T DEAD BEFORE
IT´S RAINING CATS AND DOGS
ORLANDO WASN´T DEAD BEFORE
IT´S RAINING TREES AND ROCKS

I´M A LITTLE LOVER AS THE WORLD IS PASSING BY
HELPLESS ARE WE WATCHING, CAN WE TRY?
YESTERDAY WAS GOOD ENOUGH
TO CALL ANOTHER DAY
NOW THE WORLD IS TURNING INTO GREY

I´M A LITTLE LOVER AS THE WORLD IS PASSING BY
MAYBE IT IS TIME FOR ME TO DIE
MY MOTHER AND MY FATHER
I HAVE NEVER SEEN BEFORE
THEY HIDE UP IN THE DARK AND CLOSE THE DOOR

ORLANDO WASN´T DEAD BEFORE
IT´S RAINING CATS AND DOGS
ORLANDO WASN´T DEAD BEFORE
IT´S RAINING TREES AND ROCKS

PERFECT IS YOUR LIFE

I LOVE YOU, MY DARLING
MY LOVE IS REAL
I LOVE YOU, MY DARLING
REAL LOVE I FEEL

IT IS BIGGER
THAN A GIANT IN YOUR DREAM
IT IS STRONGER
THAN THE POWERS YOU HAVE SEEN
CAUSE MY LOVE IS TRUE

AND IN A GENTLE KIND OF LIGHT
YOU UNDERSTAND PERFECT IS YOUR LIFE
YOU FOUND THE LOVING OF YOUR LIFE
I´M THE ONE FOR YOU
OUR LOVE IS RIGHT
GIRL, I LOVE YOU

I LOVE YOU, MY DARLING
MY LOVE IS STRONG
I LOVE YOU, MY DARLING
FROM THIS NIGHT ON

WE´LL BE HAPPY
LIKE 2 FLOWERS IN THE LIGHT
WE´LL BE TIGHTER
THAN THE OTHERS IN THE NIGHT
CAUSE MY LOVE IS TRUE

AND IN A GENTLE KIND OF LIGHT
YOU UNDERSTAND PERFECT IS YOUR LIFE
YOU FOUND THE LOVING OF YOUR LIFE
I´M THE ONE FOR YOU
OUR LOVE IS RIGHT
GIRL, I LOVE YOU

PIANOS IN THE NIGHT

PIANO IN THE NIGHT, PIANO IN THE NIGHT
THE DARKNESS OVERRULING THE LIGHT
PIANO IN THE NIGHT, PIANO IN THE NIGHT
THE DARKNESS OVERRULING THE LIGHT
THE WORLD IS FULL OF ANGER AND HATE
I STAND UP NOW BEFORE IT´S TOO LATE
THE PEOPLE ALL AROUND ME ARE WEAK, FEELING SMALL

PIANOS IN THE NIGHT, PIANOS IN THE NIGHT
WE NEED NOW TO UNDERSTAND THE LIGHT
PIANOS IN THE NIGHT, PIANOS IN THE NIGHT
WE NEED NOW TO UNDERSTAND THE LIGHT
THE WORLD IS FULL OF DEMONS AND LIES
I STAND UP BECAUSE I REALISE
THE PEOPLE ALL AROUND ME NEED LOVE, HERE´S MY LOVE

PIANO IN THE NIGHT KILLING DEMONS HIDING UP OUR LIGHT
PIANO IN THE NIGHT KILLS THE TRAGIC
AND YOU CAN STOP TO HIDE
PIANO IN THE NIGHT, WHITE PIANOS ALL AROUND IN THE LIGHT
WE STAND UP AND WE FIGHT
FOR SOME FREEDOM AND LOVE IN THE NIGHT

PIANO IN THE NIGHT, PIANO IN THE NIGHT
THE DARKNESS OVERRULING THE LIGHT
PIANO IN THE NIGHT, PIANO IN THE NIGHT
THE DARKNESS OVERRULING THE LIGHT
THE WORLD IS FULL OF ANGER AND HATE
I STAND UP NOW BEFORE IT´S TOO LATE
THE PEOPLE ALL AROUND ME ARE WEAK, FEELING SMALL

PIANOS IN THE NIGHT, PIANOS IN THE NIGHT
WE NEED NOW TO UNDERSTAND THE LIGHT
PIANOS IN THE NIGHT, PIANOS IN THE NIGHT
WE NEED NOW TO UNDERSTAND THE LIGHT
THE WORLD IS FULL OF DEMONS AND LIES
I STAND UP BECAUSE I REALISE
THE PEOPLE ALL AROUND ME NEED LOVE, HERE´S MY LOVE

PIANOS IN THE NIGHT KILLING DEMONS HIDING UP OUR LIGHT
PIANOS IN THE NIGHT KILL THE TRAGIC
AND YOU CAN STOP TO HIDE
PIANOS IN THE NIGHT, WHITE PIANOS ALL AROUND IN THE LIGHT
WE STAND UP AND WE FIGHT
FOR SOME FREEDOM AND LOVE IN THE NIGHT

QUASIMODO FACE

QUITE IS ALL THE LAUGHTER
FOLLOWING ME
HARD WAS MY GOOD ANSWER
DON´T YOU AGREE?

I WAS BORN A LOSER
QUASIMODO FACE
NOT 1 SENORITA
KISSED MY SPOOKY FACE

DREAMS OF LOVE IN THE NIGHT
FIGHTS OF PRIDE IN THE DAY
GUYS GET STRONG IN THE LIGHT
BUT THEY NEED TO KNOW
ALL THE MOVES OF VAN DAMME
FASTER THAN JACKIE CHAN
I KNOW ALL MARTIAL ARTS
SO YOU BETTER GO

THOUGH I HAD NO GIRLFRIEND
UP TO THIS DAY
MAYBE I WILL FIND YOU
COMING MY WAY

ONLY YOU MAY CALL ME
QUASIMODO FACE
I WILL MAKE YOU HAPPY
WITH MY SPOOKY FACE

DREAMS OF LOVE IN THE NIGHT
FIGHTS OF PRIDE IN THE DAY
GUYS GET STRONG IN THE LIGHT
BUT THEY NEED TO KNOW
ALL THE MOVES OF VAN DAMME
FASTER THAN JACKIE CHAN
I KNOW ALL MARTIAL ARTS
SO YOU BETTER GO

R - T

REGENBOGENLAND

HEY, WIE KOMMST DU
AN DAS SILBERAMULETT?
DAS ERFÜLLT 3 WÜNSCHE DIR
ES WIRD DEIN SCHATZ
WENN DU KRÄFTIG AN IHM REIBST
KOMMT DER ZAUBERER ZU DIR

HÖRST DU DIESE MELODIE?
SIE BEFREIT DICH VON DEINEN SORGEN
LEBE DEINE FANTASIEN
UND DU MUSST NICHT WARTEN AUF MORGEN

MIT DEM SILBERAMULETT
KANNST DU FLIEGEN ÜBER DEN WOLKEN
AUF INS REGENBOGENLAND
DAS KATER KARL FÜR SICH ERFAND
UND FÜR DICH

TIEF IN DER NACHT
WENN DU NICHT MEHR SCHLAFEN KANNST
SCHEINT DEIN SILBERAMULETT
BIST DU BEREIT?
WENN DU KRÄFTIG AN IHM REIBST
HOLT ES DICH AUS DEINEM BETT

AUF INS REGENBOGENLAND
WO SCHON ANDERE KIDS AUF DICH WARTEN
AB INS SCHAUKELKARUSSELL
SCHNALL DICH AN, DANN KÖNNEN WIR STARTEN

MIT DEM SILBERAMULETT
KANNST DU FLIEGEN ÜBER DEN WOLKEN
UND IM REGENBOGENLAND
DAS KATER KARL FÜR DICH ERFAND
GEHT´S DIR GUT

SANTA CLAUS IS COMING HOME

BISCUITS EVERYWHERE
SNOWBALLS IN THE AIR
CHRISTMAS TIME HAS COME
FAMILIES REUNITE, SINGLES HAVING FUN
GETTING UP AT 8
NO, I WON´T BE LATE
FOR A NIGHT OF JOY
MAYBE SANTA CLAUS WILL BE HERE TODAY

SANTA CLAUS IS COMING HOME
PRESENTS IN HIS BAGS
SANTA CLAUS IS COMING HOME
TOYS AND SWEETIE SNACKS

OUTSIDE VERY COLD
TREE IS GREEN AND GOLD
CHRISTMAS SONGS WE SING
WATCH THE CHILDREN IN ACTION, DANCE AND SING
CHRISTMAS HOLIDAY
NO ONE FLIES AWAY
SANTA´S COMING HOME
HAVE A WONDERFUL CHRISTMAS AFTERNOON!

WHAT A HOLY CHRISTMAS NIGHT
LOVE IS ALL AROUND
LET´S ENJOY THIS CHRISTMAS NIGHT
SANTA´S NOW IN TOWN

WINTER WONDERLAND
PEOPLE HAND IN HAND
SMILING ALL THE WAY
SANTA CLAUS AND HIS PRESENTS MAKE MY DAY
FIRST OF ALL THE LOVE
COMING FROM ABOVE
HEALING OUR SOULS
CHRISTMAS AFTERNOON SANTA´S COMING HOME

SCHENK MIR EINE STERNENSCHNUPPE

JA, DEIN TAG WAR WIRKLICH WUNDERSCHÖN
ZEIT IST ES FÜR DICH INS BETT ZU GEHEN
MORGEN WENN DIE SONNE FRÜH ERWACHT
WARTET SCHON AUF DICH EIN NEUER TAG

SIEHST DU AUCH DEN MOND
OBEN AM PLAFOND?

SCHENK MIR EINE STERNENSCHNUPPE
DANN SING ICH EIN LIED FÜR DICH
VON DEM SEEMANN IN DER HÜTTE
WENN DU EINMAL TRAURIG BIST
ER KANN WELLEN ÜBERQUEREN
ER SIEHT DIE STERNE
UNTER IHM DAS MEER

MÖCHTEST DU HEUT NACHT AUF REISEN GEHEN?
WIE EIN VOGEL DEINE RUNDEN DREHEN
LACHEN WEIL DU EINFACH GLÜCKLICH BIST
BIS DER NEUE TAG GEKOMMEN IST

KOMM, GIB MIR DIE HAND
AUF ZUM MÄRCHENLAND

SCHENK MIR EINE STERNENSCHNUPPE
DANN SING ICH EIN LIED FÜR DICH
VON DEM SEEMANN IN DER HÜTTE
WENN DU EINMAL TRAURIG BIST
ER KANN WELLEN ÜBERQUEREN
ER SIEHT DIE STERNE
UNTER IHM DAS MEER

SCISSORING THE SCARF

YOU SAID YOU´D PHONE ME EVERY DAY
IT´S NOT TRUE
YOU SAID YOU´D NOT BE FAR AWAY
YES, YOU DO
YOU SAID YOU´D SEND ME ALL YOUR LOVE
NIGHT AND DAY
I MUST ADMIT IT´S NOT ENOUGH
FAR AWAY

SCISSORING THE SCARF
BABY, WE ARE LOSING OUR LOVE
TOO FAR AWAY
BREAKING OUR SPELL
YOU´RE TOO FAR AWAY TO HEAR THE BELL
TO SAVE OUR LOVE
NIGHTMARES IN THE NIGHT
I PREFER TO FIGHT THE WRONG AND RIGHT
AS DARKNESS FALLS
LIES UP FROM THE START
BABY, DON´T YOU FEEL YOU BREAK MY HEART?
YOU BROKE MY HEART

YOU SAID YOU´D SHOW ME WHERE YOU ARE
PICTURE´S BLACK
LAST TIME I SAW YOU IN YOUR CAR
DRIVING BACK
GUESS YOU´RE AWAY FOR FAR TOO LONG
STILL I CARE
I HAVE NO POWER TO STAY STRONG
YOU´RE NOT THERE

SCISSORING THE SCARF
BABY, WE ARE LOSING OUR LOVE
TOO FAR AWAY
BREAKING OUR SPELL
YOU´RE TOO FAR AWAY TO HEAR THE BELL
TO SAVE OUR LOVE
NIGHTMARES IN THE NIGHT
I PREFER TO FIGHT THE WRONG AND RIGHT
AS DARKNESS FALLS
LIES UP FROM THE START
BABY, DON´T YOU FEEL YOU BREAK MY HEART?
YOU BROKE MY HEART

SHE IS COLD LIKE ICE

YOU TURN AROUND WHEN I COME
YOU´RE GOING OUT, HAVING FUN
WHO´S THIS GUY ON THE PHONE?
GUESS YOU´RE NOT ALONE
NO ANGELS OF LOVE AT MY HOME

I TURN AROUND WHEN YOU COME
SEEMS SOMEONE ELSE SHARED YOUR FUN
THERE´S THIS VOICE ON YOUR PHONE
NOW HE´S ALL ALONE
NO ANGELS OF LOVE AT HIS HOME

THE WORLD IS COLD LIKE ICE
AS YOU WALK AWAY
STRAIGHT INTO YOUR ROOM
A SHAME YOU ARE FOR THE LADIES WORLD
BREAKING EVERY RULE
YOU CRASHED MY HEART
I DON´T FEEL NO MORE
TIME TO REALISE
I LOST MY WIFE AS SHE LOST HERSELF
SHE IS COLD LIKE ICE

I TURN AROUND AS YOU GO
ON TO A PLACE FOR THE SHOW
WHILE I´M USING THE PHONE
SO I´M NOT ALONE
NO ANGELS OF LOVE AT MY HOME

THE WORLD IS COLD LIKE ICE
AS YOU WALK AWAY
STRAIGHT INTO YOUR ROOM
A SHAME YOU ARE FOR THE LADIES WORLD
BREAKING EVERY RULE
YOU CRASHED MY HEART
I DON´T FEEL NO MORE
TIME TO REALISE
I LOST MY WIFE AS SHE LOST HERSELF
SHE IS COLD LIKE ICE

SHERIFF AND LADY

MR. BRANDY WALKER, THE SHERIFF IN THIS TOWN
IS RIDING ON BILLY HORSE
AND HAUNTING DALTONS ALL AROUND
THE SHERIFF´S BIG AND STRONG
AND SO NO ONE OF THIS TOWN IS CREEPING ON

THIS IS SUSIE SAXTON, THE LADY AND THE QUEEN
HER LEGS ARE IN SHAPE AND SO IS SHE
SHE´S LOOKING QUITE SUPREME
SHE KNOWS THE DICKS IN TOWN
WON´T YOU PAY HER 50 BUCKS, SHE´LL LET YOU DOWN

BRANDY AND SUSIE, SHERIFF AND LADY
NEVER ARE GETTING CLOSE
BROTHER AND SISTER, NO ONE SHOULD KISS HER
WATCHING THE OVERDOSE
HE IS THE SHERIFF, SHE IS THE LADY
LIVING TOO FAR AWAY
BOTH OF THEM ARE RIDING ANYWAY

MR. BRANDY WALKER, THE SHERIFF OF THIS LAND
THE MAN OF THE LAW AND ORDER
WHO IS SERVING FOR HIS LAND
A SHOTGUN IN THE NIGHT AND A FIST OF DYNAMITE
HE´S ALWAYS RIGHT

LADY SUSIE SAXTON, A WOMAN BRINGING FUN
10 MINUTES OF HER ARE BETTER
THAN THE MARRIAGE BEING DONE
SHE IS THE SHINING LIGHT
WITH HER TALENT AND HER BODY IN THE NIGHT

BRANDY AND SUSIE, SHERIFF AND LADY
NEVER ARE GETTING CLOSE
BROTHER AND SISTER, NO ONE SHOULD KISS HER
WATCHING THE OVERDOSE
HE IS THE SHERIFF, SHE IS THE LADY
LIVING TOO FAR AWAY
BOTH OF THEM ARE RIDING ANYWAY
BOTH OF THEM ARE RIDING ANYWAY

SHUT UP TONIGHT!

IN MY PRETTY GARDEN A LADY STANDS AROUND
SHE´S LOOKING AT ME LIKE GOOFY
AND POINTS AT MY STEREO SOUND
SHE TELLS ME SHE DON´T LIKE IT BUT I DON´T CARE
WE´RE TALKING ABOUT MY GARDEN
SO LEAVE IT OR GET A SCARE

IN MY LITTLE GARDEN THIS LADY´S GETTING LOUD
SHE´S POINTING AT ME AND SCREAMING
I TELL HER NOW TO GET OUT
A GENTLEMAN OF NEIGHBOUR I WANT TO BE
THIS LADY IS SUCH A LOSER
NO MAN AND NO DOG I SEE

I´M TURNING AWAY
AND LEAVE HER JUST STANDING THERE
GET OUT OF MY WAY, EXPRESSING THAT I DON´T CARE
NO LOVE IN HER EYES, NO LOVE IN HER EMPTY LIFE
I´M TELLING HER NOW TO BETTER SHUT UP TONIGHT

IN MY PRETTY GARDEN I JUST ENJOY THE SUN
THE FLOWERS AROUND AND YELLOW
THE BUTTERFLIES HAVING FUN
SWEET BREAKFAST IN THE MORNING, A PLACE OF LOVE
ENJOYING THIS SCENE OF MAGIC
ENJOYING THIS PLACE OF LOVE

LADY OUT OF NOWHERE, SHE´S SCREAMING VERY LOUD
I SHOULDN´T BE HERE ENJOYING
I SHOULDN´T BE PLAYING OUT
HER FACE IS RED AND WILLING TO HIT ME MORE
A GENTLEMAN OF A NEIGHBOUR
I CANNOT BE ANYMORE

I´M TURNING AWAY
AND LEAVE HER JUST STANDING THERE
GET OUT OF MY WAY, EXPRESSING THAT I DON´T CARE
NO LOVE IN HER EYES, NO LOVE IN HER EMPTY LIFE
I´M TELLING HER NOW TO BETTER SHUT UP TONIGHT

SKY OF MAGIC

BABY, YOU KNOW IT´S BEEN SOME TIME
I WAS WITH YOU
MAYBE THE SUN RESTARTS TO SHINE
TELL ME YOU DO

I´M STILL IN LOVE WITH YOU
FOR YOU I WILL GO
AND LEAVE MY LIFE FOR SOMETHING
I SURELY KNOW

A SKY OF MAGIC TAKES MY TIME
HUH HUH
THE WORLD IS DIFFERENT, THE WORLD IS FINE
HUH HUH
AND WHEN I HOLD YOU AND TAKE YOU BACK
HUH HUH
YOU BRING THE SUNSHINE INTO MY BED

NEVER AGAIN WILL I BE CRUEL
MAKING YOU GO
NEVER AGAIN I´LL BE A FOOL
THIS ONE I KNOW

AND MAYBE YOU WILL MARRY ME
JUST ONE DAY
I SWEAR I´LL NEVER LET YOU GO
FAR AWAY

A SKY OF MAGIC TAKES MY TIME
HUH HUH
THE WORLD IS DIFFERENT, THE WORLD IS FINE
HUH HUH
AND WHEN I HOLD YOU AND TAKE YOU BACK
HUH HUH
YOU BRING THE SUNSHINE INTO MY BED

SLEEPING UP THE LADDER

SUMMER DAYS AND SUMMER NIGHTS
THE COUNTER MOVING ON
LOOKING FOR SWEET HORNY GIRLS
I TAKE THEM ONE BY ONE
A ROMEO I AM TONIGHT, A PLAYBOY IN A SUIT
I´M SLEEPING UP THE LADDER
FOR A CHANCE IN HOLLYWOOD

INFLUENCERS, INSTAGRAMERS TWITTERING THEIR LIFE
HUNDRED MILLION FOLLOWERS
THEY LIVE A BETTER LIFE
AS ROMEO THE SUPERMAN I CREEP INTO THEIR LIVES
A MAKE THEM MINE, I MAKE THEM MINE
WE´RE HAVING A GOOD TIME

INFLUENCERS, INSTAGRAMERS, I´M THE ONE FOR YOU
WANNA BE A SUPERSTAR IN HOLLYWOOD, I DO
GIVE MY BEST AND GIVE IT ALL
ON SUMMER NIGHTS AND DAYS
HOLLYWOOD, A PLAYBOY´S ON HIS WAY

HOLLYWOOD, NO BOLLYWOOD, I´M MOVING TO L.A.
LOOKING FOR RICH HORNY LADIES
MAYBE THEY ARE GREY
THE HOUR OF THE POWER MAY BE BETTER THAN A SHINE
THE MONEY BEATS THE BEAUTY
I CAN MAKE HER A GOOD TIME

AS A PLAYBOY, AS A ROMEO I´M SLEEPING UP
SLEEPING UP THE LADDER TIL THE FINAL MIGHTY SHOT
THE DAY WILL COME, THE DAY WILL COME
THE COUNTER MOVING ON
I´M SLEEPING UP THE LADDER
MAKE MY BUSINESS ONE BY ONE

INFLUENCERS, INSTAGRAMERS, I´M THE ONE FOR YOU
WANNA BE A SUPERSTAR IN HOLLYWOOD, I DO
GIVE MY BEST AND GIVE IT ALL
ON SUMMER NIGHTS AND DAYS
HOLLYWOOD, A PLAYBOY´S ON HIS WAY

SO ENDS ANOTHER LIFE

ANOTHER MAN OF 80 NOW IS DEAD
HIS WIFE JUST HAD ENOUGH
AND SHE WENT MAD
SHE KILLED HIM WITH A SHOTGUN IN THE NIGHT
WE GOT THE CALL
I REALISED THE HATE UP IN HER EYES
SHE MADE HIM FALL

AND SO NOW ENDS ANOTHER LIFE
THE MAN GOT BEAT UP BY HIS WIFE
WITHOUT YOU, WITHOUT YOU
THEY LIVED TOGETHER JUST 1 LIFE
THE MAN IS DEAD BUT NOT HIS WIFE
WITHOUT HER, WITHOUT HER

SO DEVASTATED WAS JUST HOW I FELT
THE SHOTGUN WAS STILL STUCK
IN HER RIGHT HAND
I´VE NEVER SEEN A PAIR OF GRUESOME EYES
UP IN HER FACE
SHE TOLD A QUITE HORRENDOUS IN THE NIGHT
THE STORY GOES

AND SO NOW ENDS ANOTHER LIFE
THE MAN GOT BEAT UP BY HIS WIFE
WITHOUT YOU, WITHOUT YOU
THEY SPENT TOGETHER ALL THEIR LIFE
THE MAN IS DEAD BUT NOT HIS WIFE
WITHOUT HER, WITHOUT HER

SHE IS A MURDERER FOR SURE
SHE SHOT HIM DOWN RIGHT TO THE FLOOR
LET ME OUT
OH, LET ME OUT

SO IT IS LOVE

SO IT IS LOVE
OUR FATHERS MADE THE CHOICE
20 OF AGE, OF ALL THE GIRLS AND BOYS
THEY PUT US TOGETHER LIKE BREAD AND BUTTER
WE DIDN´T HAVE ANY CHOICE TO BE TRUE
SO IT IS LOVE FROM THE DAY WE START

DIDN´T ENJOY
THE COLOUR OF YOUR FACE
PRETTY YOU ARE BUT NEVER IN A DAY
YOU WOULDN´T BE MY FIRST CHOICE IF I COULD DO
WELL, MAYBE JUST FOR A DAY OR ONE NIGHT
BUT NOT FOR SURE TIL MY DEADLY END

SO IT IS LOVE
AND I LOOK INTO YOUR EYES
SHOW ME YOUR LOVE
I AM WAITING FOR A SURPRISE
I´M SORRY FOR 2
IT´S THE OTHERS
AND SO IT IS LOVE IN THE BLUE

BIG ARE YOUR HANDS
YOUR VOICE RINGS IN MY EARS
WHITEN YOUR TEETH, I SEE YOUR FACE IN TEARS
I´M SORRY I´M NOT THE MAN OF YOUR DAYDREAMS
I´M SORRY YOU´RE NOT THE ONE IN MY MIND
SO IT IS LOVE, CAN WE GET ALONG?

SO IT IS LOVE
AND I LOOK INTO YOUR EYES
SHOW ME YOUR LOVE
I AM WAITING FOR A SURPRISE
I´M SORRY FOR 2
IT´S THE OTHERS
AND SO IT IS LOVE IN THE BLUE

SPENCER & I

PACKING MY BAGS, YOU ARRIVE ON TIME
LEAVING THIS PLACE, AS YOU WATCH I SHINE
IT´S OVER AND OUT
I WILL NEVER TURN AROUND AND SAY
„I´M SORRY FOR ALL", WELL, IT´S OVER NOW ANYWAY

SHUT UP YOUR MOUTH AND ENJOY MY FACE
LEAVING THIS HOT BUT AGGRESSIVE PLACE
I NEVER COULD BE
SUCH A CLASSY EMPTY-BRAINER MAN
A WRECKING MACHINE
WITH A BRAIN I DIDN´T UNDERSTAND

SPENCER AND I HAVE A RENDEZVOUS IN THE MORNING
IF YOU NOW THINK I´M A GAY LORD IN THE NIGHT
I´LL MAKE YOU CRY OUT LOUD
WHEN YOU SEE WHO I´M ADORING
SOME ROLLING STONES UP IN YOUR HEAD
YOU START TO CRY

7 LONG MONTH I WAS LIVING BY
7 OF ALL YOU JUST MADE ME CRY
I DIDN´T TURN LEFT
AND YOU HANDICAPPED ME TURNING RIGHT
A PRISONERS LIFE
I WAS PUSHED AROUND TOUGH AND TIGHT

NOW IT IS TIME TO UNFLAT MY WINGS
LEAVING THIS PLACE TO EXPLORE GOOD THINGS
I SEE YOU LIKE THIS
SNOBBY LADY, BETTER TAKE A BONE
I´M WAVING GOODBYE
AS YOU THROW AT ME A DIRTY STONE

SPENCER AND I HAVE A RENDEZVOUS IN THE MORNING
IF YOU NOW THINK I´M A GAY LORD IN THE NIGHT
I´LL MAKE YOU CRY OUT LOUD
WHEN YOU SEE WHO I´M ADORING
SOME ROLLING STONES UP IN YOUR HEAD
YOU START TO CRY

STALKER

I´M TURNING ON THE RADIO
AND LISTEN TO YOUR VOICE
I´M STARING AT YOUR PICTURE
MAKING MOVEMENTS OF MY CHOICE
YOU NEVER GET TO KNOW ME
I´M A STALKER IN THE DARK
YOU BETTER BE AWARE
TO NOT UNCRUCIFY MY HEART

I´M SENDING YOU A LETTER
WITH MY DIRTY DEEDS AND MORE
A PICTURE OF MY CANDY STICK
I´M SLIPPING THROUGH YOUR DOOR
I´M CALLING UP TO HEAR YOUR VOICE
SO SEXY YOUR „HELLO“
I SEE YOU TAKE A SHOWER
SO NOW WELCOME TO THE SHOW

NEVER EVER THOUGHT I´D BE A STALKER
BUT ALL THE BEAUTY I JUST SEE GIVES ME NO CHANCE
IF YOU UNLEASH MY SECRET MAYBE YOU´RE IN DANGER
WITH EVERY WORD YOU SAY

I´M HIDING IN MY PORSCHE
WITH A CAP AND GLASSES ON
I´M EATING IN THE RESTAURANT
BEFORE YOUR SALAD´S GONE
I KNOW THE GUYS YOU´RE DATING
MAKING PICTURES OF YOUR LOVE
YOU CANNOT SEE THE MINICAMS
THAT VIDEO YOUR STUFF

A STALKER IN THE MORNING
AND A STALKER IN THE NIGHT
THE FEAR I SEE IN YOUR EYES
MAKES ME HORNY DAY AND NIGHT
A MONSTER OF A KIND
TOO MANY WOMEN RUINED MY LIFE
AND SO I´M STALKING LADIES
NOW THEY HAVE TO PAY THE PRICE

NEVER EVER THOUGHT I´D BE A STALKER
BUT ALL THE BEAUTY I JUST SEE GIVES ME NO CHANCE
IF YOU UNLEASH MY SECRET MAYBE YOU´RE IN DANGER
WITH EVERY WORD YOU SAY

STERNENKIND

HINTER DER WÜSTE
DA LIEGT EIN GALAKTISCHES LAND
HINTER DER DÜNE
DAS MEER UND EIN GLITZERNDER STRAND

KAUM EINER KENNT DEN ORT
KAUM EINER WAR SCHON MAL DORT
DORT WO WIR STERNE SEHEN
DORT WO WIR ALLES VERSTEHEN

STERNENKIND
DU BIST NIEMALS ALLEIN
ICH BIN IMMER BEI DIR
WENN DU EINSAM BIST
DENK GLEICH AN MICH
UND ICH BEAM MICH ZU DIR

AUF DEINEM LEBENSWEG
WIRST DU NICHT ALLES VERSTEHEN
MANCHMAL GANZ TRAURIG
DOCH MEIST IST DAS LEBEN SEHR SCHÖN

IM GALAKTISCHEN LAND
AM GOLD GLITZERNDEN STRAND
DORT WO DIE STERNE STEHEN
HIER KANNST DU ALLES VERSTEHEN

STERNENKIND
DU BIST NIEMALS ALLEIN
ICH BIN IMMER BEI DIR
WENN DU EINSAM BIST
DENK GLEICH AN MICH
UND ICH BEAM MICH ZU DIR

STILL AIN´T READY TO GO

DOCTOR, PLEASE TELL ME THE TRUTH
HOW LONG WILL I BE AWAY?
DON´T WANNA END UP AND DIE
BUT YOUR EYES ARE TOO SAD I MUST SAY
THE PRESSURE INSIDE ME, MY POWER
IS LEAVING MY BODY FOR SURE
THE DOCTOR SAYS „SORRY", GOOD ANSWER AS HE GOES

YESTERDAY CHANGED ALL MY LIFE
FEELING A PAIN IN MY CHEST
CALLING THE 9 AND 1 1
BUT THE MEDICAL LADS WERE TOO LATE
I OPENED MY EYES HOURS LATER
A HOSPITAL ROOM I WAS IN
THE DOCTOR SAID „1 MINUTE LATER", LUCKY THING

RIGHT ON THE VERGE OF THE LIVING-OR-DYING THING
WATCHNG MY PICTURES OF LOVE
SEND ME AN MAGICAL ANGEL
THE TRAGICAL THINGS GET DESTROYED BY ABOVE
RIGHT AS THE CLOCK HITS THE 7
MY BODY IS FLYING TO HEAVEN, I GO
I AM STILL FIGHTING, A THUNDER AND LIGHTNING
IS SENDING ME STRENGTH NOW TO SHOW
STILL I AIN´T READY TO GO

HAPPY I WAS ALL MY LIFE, STILL I´M NOT READY TO GO
SO MUCH OF LIFE TO ENJOY
BUT I´M REACHING THE TOP OF MY LOW
THE DARK NOW GETS DARKER AND COLDER
THE TAKER IS STARING AT ME
AND MAYBE I HAVE ENOUGH POWER TO BE FREE

RIGHT ON THE VERGE OF THE LIVING-OR-DYING THING
WATCHNG MY PICTURES OF LOVE
SEND ME AN MAGICAL ANGEL
THE TRAGICAL THINGS GET DESTROYED BY ABOVE
RIGHT AS THE CLOCK HITS THE 7
MY BODY IS FLYING TO HEAVEN, I GO
I AM STILL FIGHTING, A THUNDER AND LIGHTNING
IS SENDING ME STRENGTH NOW TO SHOW
STILL I AIN´T READY TO GO

STILL BELIEVE I FIND YOU

ON FOR ANOTHER YEAR
FOR ANOTHER TIME
FOR ANOTHER LOVE
STONES CANNOT BREAK MY BONES
CANNOT BREAK MY HEART
I WILL FIND MY WAY

DREAMS MAY BE WRONG I KNOW
MAYBE THEY ARE CRUEL
I SHOULD HARDLY GO
LOVE EVERYBODY LIKES
EVERYBODY KNOWS
ON THE EDGE TONIGHT

I THINK I BETTER NOT RUN AWAY FROM YOU
THE CHANCE YOU COULD BE THE ONE OF MY LIFE
YOU KNOW OF THE 100 GIRLS, VANISHED MEMORIES
I SILL BELIEVE I FIND YOU IN THIS LIFE

HOPE NEVER WILL BE DEAD
NEVER TURNS AWAY
I BELIEVE IN LOVE
ON FOR ANOTHER ROAD
FOR ANOTHER CHANCE
WHILE I´M GETTING OLD

MAYBE I BETTER NOT RUN AWAY FROM YOU
THE CHANCE YOU COULD BE THE ONE OF MY LIFE
YOU KNOW OF THE 100 GIRLS, FADED MEMORIES
I SILL BELIEVE I FIND YOU IN THIS LIFE

TRUST ME, MY FRIEND
IT AIN´T CLEAR ENOUGH
I NEED TO KNOW WHAT IS LOVE
MAYBE THIS GIRL
IS THE ONE FOR ME
GUESS I WILL FIND IT OUT TONIGHT

STILL COMIN´ HOME

ANOTHER NIGHT OF YOU AND I
TAKE A SHOWER
BEFORE I HOLD YOU CLOSE
TELL ME ABOUT YOUR WORKING DAY
AND HOW IT GOES

HOW MANY GUYS DID IT TODAY?
THEY LEFT HAPPY
CAUSE I KNOW WHAT YOU ARE
I DON´T REALLY GIVE A DAMN
YOU WENT THAT FAR

CAUSE ALL I KNOW IS I´M STILL LOVING YOU
THE VERY DAY YOU WENT ALONG
I CROSSED THE LINE CAUSE I BELIEVED IN YOU
STILL COMIN´ HOME

EXHAUSTED AS YOU ARE TODAY
ALL THE PICTURES
THEY VANISH IN MY MIND
RIDIN´ AND PLAYIN´ WITH A DOG
YOU LEAVE BEHIND

ANOTHER NIGHT OF YOU AND I
YOU´RE MY LADY
MY BABY AND MY WIFE
ALL THINGS I REALLY WANNA DO
UNSHAPE MY LIFE

CAUSE ALL I KNOW IS I´M STILL LOVING YOU
THE VERY DAY YOU WENT ALONG
I CROSSED THE LINE CAUSE I BELIEVED IN YOU
STILL COMIN´ HOME

SUPERGROSSE MARSHMALLOWS

DER RIESE POLYPHEM IST NICHT ALLEIN
DRUM LÄDT ER DICH AUF SEINE INSEL EIN
SEIN BART IST LANG, ER MISST 2 METER 10
ER PFLEGT IHN MIT ´NEM RIESENGROSSEN FÖN

SEIN HAUS LIEGT AN DER KLIPPE, GLEICH AM MEER
VON HIER AUS STEUERT ER DEN SCHIFFSVERKEHR
ER ISST AM LIEBSTEN BUNTE MARSHMALLOWS
AUF SEINER INSEL, DA IST ALLES GROSS

HIER UND JETZT GIBT´S
SUPERGROSSE MARSHMALLOWS
NIMM DIR WAS DU KRIEGST
DANN IST DIE FREUDE GROSS
HIER UND JETZT GIBT´S
SUPERGROSSE MARSHMALLOWS
NIMM DIR WAS DU KRIEGST
DANN IST DIE FREUDE GROSS

EIN INSELFREUND VON POLYPHEM IST HIER
ER NENNT SICH KARL UND IST EIN PFOTENTIER
EIN KATER DER DIE MENSCHENSPRACHE KANN
ER LEBT BEIM RIESEN SCHON 2 JAHRE LANG

UND KARL, DER KATER ZEIGT DIR SEINEN SCHATZ
EIN SILBERAMULETT IN SEINER TATZ
WER KRÄFTIG DARAN REIBT WECKT AUF DEN GEIST
UND DER ERFÜLLT DIR WÜNSCHE UND ZWAR 3

KARL, DER KATER
UND DER RIESE POLYPHEM
MÖCHTEST DU DIE BEIDEN
MORGEN WIEDERSEHEN?
POLYPHEM IST GROSS
DOCH KATER KARL IST KLEIN
SIE LADEN DICH ERNEUT
AUF IHRE INSEL EIN

THE CHANCES ARE LOST

ANOTHER NIGHT IS LIKE A MIRACLE
ANOTHER NIGHT IS PASSING BY
I MUST ADMIT I´M VERY CRITICAL
I KNOW THE WORDING OF THE SKY

INTO THE CHANCES OF THE TIME
ANOTHER HEARTBEAT IN MY LIFE
THE PAST HAS NEVER BEEN BEFORE
THE FUTURE CALLS ME OUT FOR MORE

SO DEADLY YOU ARE
I´M READY TO FLEE
THE CHANCES ARE LOST
THE POWER TO SEE
I KNOW WHO YOU ARE
BUT DON´T KNOW YOUR AIM
I THINK IT COULD BE
FOR MONEY AND FAME

YOU´RE GETTING BIGGER EVERY MINUTE NOW
YOU´RE GETTING BIGGER EVERY DAY
THE WORLD IS CHANGING INTO SOMETHING NOW
I DON´T KNOW IF IT´S GOOD TO STAY

YOUR EYES ARE STRONGER THAN BEFORE
AND ALL YOUR POWER EVEN MORE
I DON´T KNOW IF IT´S GOOD TO KNOW
YOUR PLANS AND WHAT YOU DID BEFORE

SO DEADLY YOU ARE
I´M READY TO FLEE
THE CHANCES ARE LOST
THE POWER TO SEE
I KNOW WHO YOU ARE
BUT DON´T KNOW YOUR AIM
I THINK IT COULD BE
FOR MONEY AND FAME

THE DAY WILL COME

I KNOW THE DAY WILL COME
WHEN I SMILE AT YOU
I KNOW THE NIGHT WILL COME
WHEN I SLEEP WITH YOU
DON´T TELL ME WHO YOU ARE
BUT I WILL FIND IT OUT

I KNOW THE DAY WILL COME
WHEN I HOLD YOU TIGHT
I KNOW THE NIGHT WILL COME
YOU TURN OFF THE LIGHT
DON´T CALL ME ON THE PHONE
BUT I WILL FIND YOU OUT

I KNOW THE DAY WILL COME
MAYBE IN ANOTHER YEAR, MAYBE IN ANOTHER YEAR
I KNOW THE NIGHT WILL COME
YOU WILL BE MY SUPERGIRL, YOU WILL BE MY SUPERGIRL

I KNOW THE DAY WILL COME
WHEN I TAKE YOUR HAND
I KNOW THE NIGHT WILL COME
WHEN YOU UNDERSTAND
THAT POWERS IN THE SKY
PREPARE FOR US TO BE

I KNOW THE DAY WILL COME
WHEN I MARRY YOU
I KNOW THE NIGHT WILL COME
WHEN I LOOK AT YOU
AND TELL YOU ALL ABOUT
MY FEELINGS OF GOOD LOVE

I KNOW THE DAY WILL COME
MAYBE IN ANOTHER YEAR, MAYBE IN ANOTHER YEAR
I KNOW THE NIGHT WILL COME
YOU WILL BE MY SUPERGIRL, YOU WILL BE MY SUPERGIRL

THE GOLDEN RING

WHERE´S THE GOLDEN RING
I FOUND DEEP UNDER A TREE?
I PUT IT IN A LITTLE BLACK BOX
UNDERNEATH MY BED
I CANNOT FIND ANYMORE
GUESS SOMEONE MUST HAVE TAKEN AWAY

WHERE´S THE GOLDEN RING
I FOUND DEEP UNDER A TREE?
I FELT THE MIGHTY POWERS I HAD
KNOWLEDGE OF THE DEAD
A STRONG MYSTERIOUS FORCE
I NEVER EVER WAS STRONG LIKE THAT

I SWEAR I´M GONNA FIND OUT THE TRUTH
I´D RATHER GET CRAZY
I´M COMING AFTER AND HAUNTING YOU
BEFORE YOU´RE AWAY
I NEED TO KNOW WHAT IS WRONG WITH YOU
AND IF IT´S A LADY
I´LL DO THE THINGS THAT I HAVE TO DO
AND YOU´RE GONNA PAY

WHERE´S THE GOLDEN RING
I FOUND DEEP UNDER A TREE?
A THIEF LIKE YOU WILL NEVER BE CAUGHT
AS YOU RUN AWAY
I TAPE MY FIST AS THEY SAY
THE HAUT IS ON, I´LL GET YOU TODAY!

I SWEAR I´M GONNA FIND OUT THE TRUTH
I´D RATHER GET CRAZY
I´M COMING AFTER AND HAUNTING YOU
BEFORE YOU´RE AWAY
I NEED TO KNOW WHAT IS WRONG WITH YOU
AND IF IT´S A LADY
I´LL DO THE THINGS THAT I HAVE TO DO
AND YOU´RE GONNA PAY

THIS COKE OF MINE

I DRINK A COKE OF MINE
I DRINK A COKE OF MINE
DON´T YOU DARE TO SAY A WORD
DON´T LIKE YOUR MANGO JUICE
DON´T LIKE YOUR MANGO JUICE
DON´T LOOK AT ME JUST LIKE A NERD
I DRINK IT LIGHT AND COLD
I DRINK IT LIGHT AND COLD
BETTER DON´T LOOK AT ME LIKE THIS
DON´T WANNA SEE YOUR FACE
DON´T WANNA SEE YOUR FACE, MY MANGO MISS

THOUGH YOU´RE MY WIFE I DON´T LIKE
YOU TAKIN´ CARE OF MY LIFE
I´M WILLING AND ABLE TO DRINK
NOW THIS COKE OF MINE
DON´T SHAKE YOUR HEAD, GO AWAY
SPARKLING COOL MAKES MY DAY
ENJOYING THIS MAGIC WITHOUT MY SWEET MANGO WIFE

I DRINK THIS COKE OF MINE
I DRINK THIS COKE OF MINE
COKE I WANT TO START MY DAY
DON´T LIKE NO MANGO JUICE
DON´T LIKE NO MANGO JUICE
LADY, NOW LET ME DRINK AWAY
THE BLACK IS COLD LIKE ICE
THE BLACK IS COLD WITH ICE
MOMENTS OF LOVE AND JOY I FEEL
I DRINK THIS COKE OF MINE
I DRINK THIS COKE OF MINE, WE HAVE A DEAL

THOUGH YOU´RE MY WIFE I DON´T LIKE
YOU TAKIN´ CARE OF MY LIFE
I´M WILLING AND ABLE TO DRINK
NOW THIS COKE OF MINE
DON´T SHAKE YOUR HEAD, GO AWAY
SPARKLING COOL MAKES MY DAY
ENJOYING THIS MAGIC WITHOUT MY SWEET MANGO WIFE

THIS GIRL

THIS GIRL I HAVEN´T SEEN BEFORE
THIS GIRL MAKES ME CRY
THIS PLACE I HAVEN´T BEEN BEFORE
THIS PLACE MAKES ME DIE

THIS GIRL I HAVEN´T TOUCHED BEFORE
THIS GIRL TURNS AWAY
THE TRUTH IS SHE´S NOT OUT FOR MORE
I´M LOSING MY WAY

DRINKING WHISKY
AND A LEMON LIGHT
I NEED TO KNOW
SOMEONE TELL ME
WHY THIS CRAZY GIRL
PFERERS TO GO
A HEARTBREAK KID
I´VE BEEN BEFORE
A HEARTBREAK KID
I AM NO MORE

THIS GIRL I HAVEN´T … BEFORE
THIS GIRL IS TOO SHY
THIS SO-CALLED LOST I CAN´T IGNORE
DON´T WANT ME TO CRY

DRINKING WHISKY
AND A LEMON LIGHT
I NEED TO KNOW
SOMEONE TELL ME
WHY THIS CRAZY GIRL
PFERERS TO GO
A HEARTBREAK KID
I´VE BEEN BEFORE
A HEARTBREAK KID
I AM NO MORE

THIS IS A LIE

THIS IS A LIE
THIS IS A LIE YOU SAY
COLD IS YOUR HEART
I WANNA GO AWAY
BUT THEN YOU CLOSE THE DOOR
AND SAY YOU LIE NO MORE

SHAMELESS YOU ARE
SHAMELESS YOU ARE TO ME
BREAKING MY HEART
WHERE IS A PLACE TO BE?
IS THERE A WAY TO GO
OUT OF THIS CREEPY SHOW?

WELL, MAYBE I WAS BLIND
AND MAYBE I WAS A FOOL
LIKE A FLY GET CAUGHT
I DIDN´T UNDERSTAND
I ALWAYS BELIEVED IN YOU
LOST THE FIGHT I FOUGHT

SHOWING ME UP
MAKING ME DOWN AGAIN
„HONEY“ YOU SAY
POISON YOU GIVE YOUR MAN
I QUIT TO BE WITH YOU
DON´T WANNA STAY WITH YOU

WELL, MAYBE I WAS BLIND
AND MAYBE I WAS A FOOL
LIKE A FLY GET CAUGHT
I DIDN´T UNDERSTAND
I ALWAYS BELIEVED IN YOU
LOST THE FIGHT I FOUGHT

TIME IS ON MY SIDE AS SHE´S GETTING OLD
GLORIOUS THE DAY WHEN I GO
NO MORE BUNCH OF LIES I WILL HEAR AGAIN
AS I FIND MY WAY THROUGH THE DOOR

U - Z

USB

IT´S NEVER BEEN AN EASY LIFE TO LIVE WITH YOU
IT´S NEVER BEEN AN EASY TIME TO GO
THE LOVE WE SHARED
WAS NEVER REALLY STRONG ENOUGH
TO HIGH THE LOW

A BROTHER-AND-A-SISTER-LIKE RELATIONSHIP
DON´T ASK ME NOW TO MASTURBATE WITH YOU
I´VE GOT A GOOD COLLECTION
ON MY MASTERSTICK
IT´S WITHOUT YOU

USB – MY WORLD KEEPS MOVING ON
SHOWING ME THE THINGS
ALL THE YEARS ARE DEAD AND GONE
USB – MY WORLD IS FULL OF LOVE
READ MY LIPS, BE TOUGH NOW
CAUSE YOU´VE NEVER BEEN ENOUGH

IT´S NEVER BEEN AN EASY TIME TO SLEEP WITH YOU
YOU DIDN´T HAD THE TALENT TO BE QUEEN
I SHOWED YOU LOTS OF PORN
AND TOLD YOU HOW TO DO
THE SWEET 16

I NEVER REALLY THOUGHT YOU COULDN´T UNDERSTAND
THE PICTURES FULL OF MOTION IN YOUR FACE
I SHOWED YOU HOW TO DO IT
WITH A SPEEDY HAND
UP IN YOUR FACE

USB – MY WORLD KEEPS MOVING ON
SHOWING ME THE THINGS
ALL THE YEARS ARE DEAD AND GONE
USB – MY WORLD IS FULL OF LOVE
READ MY LIPS, BE TOUGH NOW
CAUSE YOU´VE NEVER BEEN ENOUGH

WAS IST HIER LOS?

ICH DÜS AUF DER AUTOBAHN VON MÜNCHEN NACH BERLIN
LASSE ALLE AUTOS HINTER MIR, IST DAS NICHT SCHÖN?
PLÖTZLICH DRÄNGT MICH SO EIN DICKER
PORSCHE AB NACH RECHTS
SOWAS MACHT MICH WÜTEND, IST MIR GAR NICHT RECHT

ICH SPRING INS BÜRÖ
DOCH ALLE SCHAUEN MICH SELTSAM AN
MEINE FRISE SITZT UND MEINE HOSEN HAB ICH AN
GABI ZEIGT AUF MICH UND FLÜSTERT KLAUSI WAS INS OHR
HIMMEL, ARSCH UND ZWIRN! WAS HABEN DIE BEIDEN VOR?

WAS IST HIER LOS? WAS IST HIER LOS?
WAS IST HIER LOS? WAS IST HIER LOS?
ICH FRAG MICH BLOSS: WAS IST HIER LOS?

JA, ICH HAB ´NE FRAU
DOCH MANCHMAL GEH ICH INS BORDELL
KAUFE MIR ´NE FRAU UND DANN
VERSCHWIND ICH WIEDER SCHNELL
DIESMAL SCHÄUMT DER MOTOR
UND MEIN AUTO EXPLODIERT
FOTO IN DER ZEITUNG, HAB MICH SEHR BLAMIERT

NACH DER SCHEIDUNG GÖNN ICH MIR
´NE REISE AUF DER SEE
LIEGE IN DER SONNE UND VERGNÜGE MICH MIT SCHNEE
PLÖTZLICH KOMMT ´NE WELLE
MACHT ´NE DELLE IN DAS SCHIFF
ALLE SAUFEN AB, SO EINER RETTE MICH!

WAS IST HIER LOS? WAS IST HIER LOS?
WAS IST HIER LOS? WAS IST HIER LOS?
ICH FRAG MICH BLOSS: WAS IST HIER LOS?

WENN DANN EINES TAGES NUN DER TEUFEL NACH MIR RUFT
DREH ICH IHM ´NE NASE
DENN ICH HAB ´N SCHNELLEN FUSS
EVA WARTET NÄMLICH SCHON AUF MICH IM PARADIES
LEIDER RUTSCH ICH AB UND FALLE HÖLLISCH TIEF

WHERE IS THE GIRL I LOVE?

SEE THE STARS IN MY ROOM
FEEL THE LIGHT OF THE STARS
TAKE THE STARS IN YOUR HAND
LET THEM FLY AWAY

HEAR THE WORDS OF MY HEART
LIVE AND PRAY TO THE WORDS
HOLD THE WORDS IN YOUR HANDS
LET THEM FLY AGAIN

LUCKILY THE LADY IN PARADISE
HER EYES ARE BRIGHT AND READY TO SHINE
I KNOW THE TRUTH IS NEVER ENDLESS
HER PRETTY FACE CAN CHANGE THE WORLD
I´M SPENDING MY TIME
IT ISN´T CLEAR ENOUGH
WHERE IS THE GIRL I LOVE?

STAY WITH ME TIL THE END
TIL THE END OF MY LIFE
IF MY LIFE WILL BE SHORT
MAKE ME STAY ALIVE

GIVE YOUR LOVE TO THE ONE
I´M THE ONE JUST FOR YOU
CAN YOU FEEL OUR LOVE
STRONGER THAN OUR LIVES?

LUCKILY THE LADY IN PARADISE
HER EYES ARE BRIGHT AND READY TO SHINE
I KNOW THE TRUTH IS NEVER ENDLESS
HER PRETTY FACE CAN CHANGE THE WORLD
I´M SPENDING MY TIME
IT ISN´T CLEAR ENOUGH
WHERE IS THE GIRL I LOVE?

WHERE´S THIS GIRL I´VE SEEN AROUND THIS POOL?

I SAW YOU THERE AROUND THIS POOL
I COULDN´T TAKE MY EYES
OFF YOU ANOTHER WAY
I REALISE I WAS A FOOL
I DIDN´T TAKE THE CHANCE BUT RAN AWAY

MAYBE I WILL SEE YOU ONCE AGAIN
MAYBE YOU´RE MY GIRL AND I´M YOUR MAN
AND WE´LL BE CLOSE LIKE IN A DREAM

WHERE´S THIS GIRL I´VE SEEN AROUND THIS POOL?
I GIVE MY WORD, NEXT TIME I´M NOT A FOOL
GIVE ME A CHANCE TO FIND MY LOVE
I WILL KISS HER AND I´M GONNA SAY:
I´M SO IN LOVE WITH YOU, DON´T GO AWAY
GIVE ME A CHANCE TO SHOW MY LOVE

YOU HYPNOTIZED MY BROKEN HEART
WITHOUT A WORD YOU SAID
BUT WITH YOUR PURPLE EYES
I FELL FOR YOU BUT LOST THE START
I´M GONNA FIND YOU FOR A BIG SURPRISE

I WILL TAKE YOU EVERYWHERE I GO
IF YOU KNOW ME EVERYTHING I KNOW
THAT OUR LOVE WILL REACH THE SUN

WHERE´S THIS GIRL I´VE SEEN AROUND THIS POOL?
I GIVE MY WORD, NEXT TIME I´M NOT A FOOL
GIVE ME A CHANCE TO FIND MY LOVE
I WILL KISS YOU AND I´M GONNA SAY:
I´M SO IN LOVE WITH YOU, DON´T GO AWAY
GIVE ME A CHANCE TO SHOW MY LOVE

IN MY DREAMS I SEE YOU EVERY NIGHT
IN MY DREAMS I HUG AND HOLD YOU TIGHT
ANOTHER DAY YOU WILL BE MINE

WHILE YOU´RE AWAY

IT´S BEEN A LONG AND LONELY TIME
NO WORD OF YOU WHILE YOU´RE AWAY
THE CLOCK IS RUNNING, PASSING BY
IT SEEMS SO ENDLESS
I´M GETTING OLDER IN MY TIME
WHILE YOU´RE AWAY

IS THERE ANOTHER BUNCH OF MEN?
AND MAYBE I WILL FIND IT OUT
SO MANY HOURS YOU´RE AWAY
IT DRIVES ME SENSELESS
I´M LOOKING FORWARD TO THE DAY
YOU´RE COMING HOME

HONESTLY
10 HOURS YOU´RE AWAY NOW
WORKING AT YOUR OFFICE, I´M ALONE
HONESTLY
I KNOW IT´S JUST 10 HOURS
FEELING LIKE 10 YEARS YOU´RE FAR FROM HOME

A MOOD OF MYSTERY IN MY MIND
HOW CAN IT BE TIME RUNS SO SLOW?
I PLAY THE STATION IN THE DARK
SOME LONELY HOURS
THE TIME OF WAITING CAN BE HARD
WHILE YOU´RE AWAY

HONESTLY
10 HOURS YOU´RE AWAY NOW
WORKING AT YOUR OFFICE, I´M ALONE
HONESTLY
I KNOW IT´S JUST 10 HOURS
FEELING LIKE 10 YEARS YOU´RE FAR FROM HOME

WUNDERSCHÖNER TAG

ES WAR EIN WUNDERSCHÖNER TAG
JETZT DARFST DU SCHLAFEN GEHEN
JA, MORGEN BIN ICH WIEDER DA
ABER JETZT TRÄUME SCHÖN
VERSPROCHEN, WIR WERDEN UNS WIEDERSEHEN

DER SANDMANN IST MEIN BESTER FREUND
SEI BRAV UND HÖR IHM ZU
SCHLIESS DEINE AUGEN, SEI BEREIT
IN DEINER FANTASIE, DA FLIEGST DU
UND LANDEST MORGEN FRÜH

ES WAR EIN WUNDERSCHÖNER TAG
JA, MORGEN BIN ICH WIEDER FÜR DICH DA
DER SANDMANN SCHENKT DIR EINEN TRAUM
DER ZAUBER IN DER NACHT BESCHERT DIR
MORGEN EINEN WUNDERSCHÖNEN TAG
ICH SCHLAFE EIN

HEUT WIRD EIN WUNDERSCHÖNER TAG
DIE SONNE STRAHLT DICH AN
DU ISST ZUM FRÜHSTÜCK WAS DU MAGST
ES SCHMECKT SO GUT UND DANN
ZEIG ICH DIR WAS DIESER TAG SO KANN

WIR KÖNNEN TOBEN, KÖNNEN SPIELEN
BIS UNS GANZ SCHWINDLIG WIRD
WIR KÖNNEN SINGEN, MUSIZIEREN
MIT DIESER MELODIE
DIE STUNDEN MIT DIR VERGESS ICH NIE

ES WAR EIN WUNDERSCHÖNER TAG
JA, MORGEN BIN ICH WIEDER FÜR DICH DA
DER SANDMANN SCHENKT DIR EINEN TRAUM
DER ZAUBER IN DER NACHT BESCHERT DIR
MORGEN EINEN WUNDERSCHÖNEN TAG
ICH SCHLAFE EIN